Country Home.

# new country
## style

Country Home. Books
Des Moines, Iowa

**COUNTRY HOME® BOOKS**
An imprint of Meredith® Books

**NEW COUNTRY STYLE**
Editor: VICKI L. INGHAM
Associate Design Director: KEN CARLSON
Contributing Writers: CYNTHIA PEARSON ADAMS, DEBRA LANDWEHR FELTON, KARIN BAJI HOLMS
Copy Chief: CATHERINE HAMRICK
Copy and Production Editor: TERRI FREDRICKSON
Book Production Managers: PAM KVITNE, MARJORIE J. SCHENKELBERG
Contributing Copy Editor: CAROL BOKER
Contributing Proofreaders: SUSAN J. KLING, BETH LASTINE, NANCY RUHLING, M. PEG SMITH
Indexer: ELIZABETH T. PARSON
Electronic Production Coordinator: PAULA FOREST
Editorial and Design Assistants: KAYE CHABOT, MARY LEE GAVIN, KAREN SCHIRM

**MEREDITH® BOOKS**
Editor in Chief: JAMES D. BLUME
Design Director: MATT STRELECKI
Managing Editor: GREGORY H. KAYKO
Executive Shelter Editor: DENISE L. CARINGER

Director, Retail Sales & Marketing: TERRY UNSWORTH
Director, Sales, Special Markets: RITA MCMULLEN
Director, Sales, Premiums: MICHAEL A. PETERSON
Director, Sales, Retail: TOM WIERZBICKI
Director, Book Marketing: BRAD ELMITT
Director, Operations: GEORGE A. SUSRAL
Director, Production: DOUGLAS M. JOHNSTON

Vice President, General Manager: JAMIE L. MARTIN

***COUNTRY HOME® MAGAZINE***
Editor in Chief: CAROL SHEEHAN
Creative Director: MARY EMMERLING
Executive Editor: JEAN SCHISSEL NORMAN

**MEREDITH PUBLISHING GROUP**
President, Publishing Group: STEPHEN M. LACY
Vice President, Finance & Administration: MAX RUNCIMAN

**MEREDITH CORPORATION**
Chairman and Chief Executive Officer: WILLIAM T. KERR

Chairman of the Executive Committee: E. T. MEREDITH III

All of us at Country Home® Books are dedicated to providing you with information and ideas to enhance your home.
We welcome your comments and suggestions. Write to us at Country Home, Shelter Editorial Department,
1716 Locust St., Des Moines, IA 50309-3023.
If you would like to purchase any of our books, check wherever quality books are sold. Visit us at www.countryhomemagazine.com.

When the United States celebrated its bicentennial in 1976, there was a tremendous surge of interest in the customs and traditions of the American past, and particularly in the homes and furnishings of our ancestors. A new appreciation emerged for the simplicity and utility found in the dwellings of the countryside, from humble farmsteads, camps, and cottages to more imposing Georgian or Victorian homes. All of these kinds of houses seemed to be imbued with values and standards we associate with rural life—a sense of rootedness and a connection to place, an appreciation for nature and the land, a love of family, and an inventive self-reliance that turns making do with what you have into a celebration of the honest beauty of simple materials. Young Americans aspired to bring the look and feeling of a country home into their own living spaces. *Country Home*® magazine was an early and important interpreter of that decorating style.

Since that time, *Country Home*® has continued to follow and report on all aspects of country style, from rustic furnishings and folk art to textiles, antiques, and crafts. In the past decade especially, the magazine has noted the gradual evolution of country home style into a wide range of looks, each one of them fresh and original. Perhaps the main reason for this rich diversity in country style has been the influx and influence of so many creative designers, dealers, decorators, artisans, and homeowners who have embraced the style while bringing their individual tastes to bear on it.

Drawing on the magazine's leadership role in chronicling styles and trends, *New Country Style* is the first book to bring together these myriad expressions. For, although firmly anchored in the past, this look is also modern at its core. The very sensibilities that women of earlier eras embraced—honesty, simplicity, practicality, and beauty—are still relevant to the way we need and want to live and to decorate our homes today, albeit in a more casual and contemporary manner—a new country style in step with the new century. I am confident that you will find *New Country Style* an invaluable and friendly guide for all your decorating projects.

*Carol Sheehan*

EDITOR IN CHIEF, *COUNTRY HOME*® MAGAZINE

*New Country Style* presents many looks, all united by an abiding love for the unique charms and comforts of the country home. I feel at home in all of these looks. And I can assure you that wherever you live, you'll find the decorating ideas in this book relevant and appealing too.

Two decades ago, the country look was basically a period interpretation of Early American style. Now there is a new design movement afoot, one that values ease, comfort, casualness, and personal expression. More than ever before, the hallmarks and ideals of country life offer an antidote to the high-tech, high-stress worlds in which we live. Our homes are now havens, and practitioners of country style have been quick to adapt, pulling up the rugs, clearing out the clutter, and applying new color palettes to walls, furnishings, and floors.

New Country Style explores these exciting new directions. The section titled New Blue takes you into living spaces enriched by antiques and country collections that have been pared down to the bare essentials, illustrating how timely and contemporary this classic look can be. In the Cottage section, flea market finds and family heirlooms mix with vintage collections for a look that's young at heart and surprising. The section called Rustic takes its inspiration from a countryside shaped by twigs, sticks, barn boards, and logs, where modern pioneers carry on the rustic tradition with verve and conviction. The Personal section showcases the trendsetters who are mining the archives of the 20th century for highly individualized looks that, while breaking all the rules, still convey the essence of country design. Who would have thought you would find mid-20th-century chairs around a farmhouse table? It's a new world out there, shaped by the evolving marketplace.

I've had great fun drawing on the ideas in this book to renew my own country home. I hope you will, too.

*Mary Emmerling*

CREATIVE DIRECTOR, *COUNTRY HOME*® MAGAZINE

# new blue

# cottage

# rustic

# personal

**Picture rows of classic white** ironstone on steel utility shelving, practical recessed lighting in an old plank ceiling, easy-cleaning glass resting on carpenter-made trestles, or a single bare bulb lighting a harvest table. New blue interiors carry the pure and simple values of our forefathers into the present day, mixing the true-blue style of country roots with new handcrafts and hardworking industrial materials. Poured concrete, corrugated iron, and galvanized steel are as much a part of country construction today as timber and stone were two centuries ago. Blending new and old into a seamless whole is also a pioneering, make-do solution to the challenge of furnishing homes. Lifestyles have changed along with the market, and

# new blue

what was used a century ago may no longer be available, affordable, or even comfortable. For country to offer refuge from urban living, ease and simplicity are key. Spaces are airy, windows undressed, and furnishings limited to what's useful or beautiful. This leaves room for heirlooms to resonate their history, and open space to echo the great outdoors. Colors are drawn from nature, but in brighter hues than before: ocean blues, seashell pinks, apple greens, grain yellows, and autumn reds and oranges. Like the contemporary artisan creating traditional handcrafts, new blue style redefines what in today's world has the honesty, strength, and integrity of the past.

# big style country

In her search for land on which to create a family retreat, Nancy Dickenson fell in love with the verdant Ocate Valley in the high desert of northern New Mexico. There she found Twin Willows Ranch, with three picturesque buildings that reflected the region's vernacular architecture. Inspired by the limitless sky and broad fields of straw-colored bromegrass, Nancy envisioned a home that would honor the vintage Southwestern style of the existing buildings and capture the serenity of the place. Santa Fe architect Laban Wingert responded by designing a long, low-lying dwelling that makes honest use of simple materials. Outside, stuccoed walls and the tin roof are unadorned. Inside, earth-colored concrete floors, rough plastered walls, and plank ceilings pay homage to the region's architectural heritage.

In the living area, furniture is streamlined in shape but scaled large to suit the overriding sense of spaciousness. White and concrete surfaces can change from cool to warm depending on the height of the sun and the season, while woven Navajo textiles and regional folk art from around the world inject an earthy palette of browns and reds into the neutral color scheme. Nancy's quirky choice of an old coffin gurney for a coffee table rounds out the mix with humor. When questioned about using modern materials like continued on page 14

OPPOSITE: **In concert with the spirit of the minimalist architecture, furnishings are few and well-chosen: Woods are limited to pale and honey tones, and upholstery throughout the house is confined to the same brushed beige cotton fabric. Instead of a permanent installation for photography, built-in ledges allow the collection to rotate and grow.** RIGHT: **Only a few years old, the adobe ranch house looks as though it has been part of the valley for generations. Landscaping involves only natural grasses and the mountainscape beyond.** FAR RIGHT: **Nancy raises quarter horses and Black Angus cattle at Twin Willows Ranch.**

Furniture that sports wheels aids the living room's flexible floor plan: Seating can be moved as needed to create a variety of configurations. Concrete floors have an earthy color reminiscent of the great outdoors and are hard-wearing, a practical choice for a working ranch. Woven ethnic throws and textiles warm up the white environment with touches of color, leading the eye to an updated version of an inglenook and the fire's warm glow. A gurney-turned-coffee table is a humorous take on the country tradition of making do.

chrome and glass on a working ranch, Nancy wisely answers, "This isn't industrial chic. It's a mix of things that feel right at home in

the country."

Nancy makes a connection between the sparseness of the house and the vastness of the countryside, which is naturally "minimal."

"Your eyes aren't darting from one thing to the next," she explains, "unlike everyday life, which bombards us with so much." Days

on the ranch can get hectic indeed, between raising performance quarter horses and Black Angus cattle and hosting a variety of

visitors, including children, grandchildren, friends, and horse breeders. Making light and space a priority offers refuge for all.

OPPOSITE: Decorated in whites, the master bath reflects an aesthetic that's vintage yet modern. The claw-foot tub and classic armchair are new. Privacy is not an issue, so the window was built wide to soak in the mountain view. BELOW: The basin is set into a concrete countertop on a vanity that floats in the middle of the bathroom. A gooseneck chrome faucet and vintage-style adjustable shaving mirror add graceful curves to soften the minimalist design.

A spacious kitchen that stretches the full width of the house can accommodate a herd of guests seated in barrel-shape leather equipale chairs at the 12-foot-long custom-made farm table. Built-in appliances and an expanse of concrete countertops contribute to the room's sleek look; open shelving keeps tableware conveniently within reach, and touch-latch cabinetry stashes everything else out of sight. The canoe model, found in Santa Fe, offers both a focal point and a nod to the room's clever blend of cowboy casual and formal symmetry.

## room for collectibles

Although the overriding mood of Nancy's home is serenely spare, she also enjoys collectibles that reflect her fondness for dogs, horses, and cowboy culture. Here's how she displays them.

• Kitschy ceramic statues of dogs line up on an antique American Empire-style dresser in the bedroom.

• A vintage pillow provides a splash of color against white quilted pillow shams.

• Cowboy-themed items, including a child's lamp and a footstool covered in cowboy-print fabric, serve practical and decorative purposes in the bedroom.

• Nancy likes to create little habitats for favorite objects. A dog-decorated container holding a cluster of roses pairs up with a vintage dog-grooming brush.

# rugged individualism

There were round windows, elliptical windows, and an oddly symmetrical facade with two sets of sliding glass doors—one set drywalled over on the inside only. The front half of the building was resting on dirt without a foundation. "It was such an oddball thing," says architect Brian Boyle, recalling his first impression of the Long Island house he had been hired to renovate. "We thought maybe it had been a barn," he says, "then it was turned into a house. We were captivated."

The former owners were local potato farmers. Boyle's client was a Wall Street executive who bought the property as a fresh-air retreat. To accommodate his needs, Boyle opened up the house to light and the landscape. He found space on the ground floor for a large great-room by moving mechanicals to a new basement dug by the foundation contractor. Next, he enlarged existing windows and added French doors on three sides of the house. But his client wanted more. Attracted to the cobbled-together structure for its folksy appeal, he encouraged Boyle to "think quirky."

Boyle responded by adding two more large windows on the second story and two exterior sliding barn doors, each with its own tiny rectangular windows, to cover screen doors. At the living area end of the great-room he added an unusually low row of five small windows to give those seated on the couch a view of the owner's beloved gardens. Outside, he added a deck

OPPOSITE: **A fresh color palette, ranging from sky blue to apple green to buttery yellow, softens the rustic effect of old floor boards and other materials used throughout the house. Using different hues in the guest bedroom, master bedroom, and connecting sitting room gives each space its own personality, unified by a single trim color.** RIGHT: **Opening the doors at one end of the great-room creates an impromptu porch. The flaking paint on an old plank rocker echoes the peeling bark on a white birch tree.** FAR RIGHT: **Outdoor dining is encouraged with three sides of the house open to the landscape via French doors.**

**BELOW LEFT AND RIGHT:** Architecture defines two views of the sitting room. The restored fireplace is now a functioning focal point. The original window was enlarged by the architect to allow more light into the cozy space. On the wall, re-engineered metal downspouts from the original roof serve as one-of-a-kind sconces. **OPPOSITE:** An old handwrought iron factory gear makes a dramatic chandelier in the double-story entrance corridor, where plastered walls and salvaged wood create a rustic look. Near the door, an old chalk baseball scoreboard hangs as art.

that slopes with the land like a ramp. Inside, Boyle put a more contemporary, lofty spin on the make-do architecture, using exposed brick and an entire barn's worth of salvaged chestnut wood planks for decorative effect on ceilings, floors, and closet doors.

When interior designer Zina Glazebrook came on the job, she took cues from the airy layout and simple materials. She laid woven rugs on the plank floors and limited furnishings to a few carefully selected pieces in earth tones and whites. "Space is its own luxury," she says. "It heightens your appreciation of a piece of furniture, a folk art object, or an architectural detail." This time the owner might have been content, but Glazebrook wanted more. She pushed for nature-based paint colors to help soften the roughness of old wood and brick. The result, she explains, was a happy marriage as "the strong architecture met soft, bright color to become even stronger."

Designed to recall the feeling of an old general store, the kitchen cabinetry is chock-full of modern conveniences, such as a built-in bin for storing wine. The new vintage-style drawer pulls and soapstone countertops are a throwback to earlier times, while the commercial range is a high-tech version of an old cook stove. Baskets hanging from the beamed ceiling recall old-fashioned keeping rooms. A painting by Howard Finster provides an arresting focal point.

## salvaged wood

When recycling wood, consider how to use it. Here chestnut planks from a North Carolina tobacco barn give a variety of effects.

• The worn, whitewashed exterior side of the wood was installed face out on doors to complement walls of salvaged bricks.

• Ceilings and floors show the reverse, or interior, side of these same planks. The floorboards shine from a clear gloss sealer, while the untreated ceiling planks appear bleached and raw.

• Brian Boyle advises looking for lumber at least ¾ inch thick and using it for decorative, not structural, purposes. Old planks can cover a ceiling's structural beams, for instance. Search for salvage companies online or in wood magazines, or call your local demolition contractors.

OPPOSITE CLOCKWISE FROM TOP: A sisal runner on the staircase sharpens the contrast between the hall's rough-hewn beams and high-gloss white paint. The house, probably a converted barn, had quirky windows and a symmetrical double entrance. A barn-style door was installed to slide over screen doors. A door fashioned from salvaged barn boards still showing layers of old whitewash conceals under-the-stairwell storage. Several styles of reclaimed architectural moldings were combined to make the great-room mantel. A simple row of collected shells and an old carved wood boat anchor call attention to the area's nautical heritage.

Playing to the scale of the furnishings in the wide expanse of the great-room, interior designer Zina Glazebrook lined three diminutive French Canadian rush-seat chairs along a wall and tucked another under the tavern-style coffee table. The sofa and club chair are, by contrast, broad and welcoming, with deep backs and ample pillows in plush natural fabrics. Overhead, the newly installed old wood beams and planks hide supporting steel spans and recessed ceiling lights. Boyle says, "We could get away with the dark wood ceiling because there was so much more natural light than before."

# pure & simple

During the week, Mark and Lisa McCormick and their two children live in a home decorated with folk art and fine antiques. On the weekends, however, they're in Amish country, the heart of simplicity itself. The couple, both antiques dealers, came across a circa-1890s farmhouse—a plain, two-bedroom structure with metal roof and tar paper siding near Belle Rive, Illinois. More than offering a weekend getaway, the house seemed to promise an old-fashioned, simpler style of life.

The house was "scary" when they first saw it, Lisa admits. "It was dirty and smelled bad." When Mark walked through it, however, he saw that it had integrity. "It was a very honest house, very simple," he says. The renovation took place over time, as the couple scraped and painted, shored up and straightened floors, evicted termites, and updated the plumbing. Then the decorating began.

The farmhouse is arguably the very epitome of American country, with few keepsakes to dust and only a few pieces of furniture that just get better with use and wear. "There's something heartwarming about all these comfortable old usable things. They slow you down and make you feel peaceful and at home," Lisa says.

Going to as many as six auctions and flea markets a day, the couple collected simple accessories. A straw hat and a birdhouse, for instance, create a still life in a bedroom. Mark found shutters at an antiques fair in Maine and installed them in the windows in lieu

OPPOSITE: Lisa chose all-wood living room pieces for weekend living. Upholstery would have been too tempting for field mice. "The Adirondack chairs are surprisingly good for lounging, especially with lots of ticking pillows on them," says Lisa. RIGHT: The McCormicks had to rebuild the entire front porch. Thanks to Mark's sister, they could do it in vintage style, using simple columns from a house she had torn down.

of curtains. A pointed Gothic window frame from an old church stands in a corner for decoration. A wide-mouthed canning jar serves as a vase for a floral bouquet. And tools, such as ladders and rakes, reminders of the farm past, take on new life as decorations throughout the house.

The Amish neighbors often stopped by during the renovation and remarked on what good workers the McCormicks were. Like their neighbors, the couple embraces simplicity as a way of life—at least for the weekends. "When you're out in the yard and the buggies are clip-clopping by," says Mark, "there's not a hint that it isn't 1910."

OPPOSITE: **A Modern Kitchens sign lends graphic appeal and irony to the old-fashioned farmhouse kitchen. The painted table and chairs are good choices for a weekend home—the family can use them indoors or out.** BELOW: **The kitchen is outfitted and furnished with country classics reminiscent of the 1930s—a galvanized countertop, sturdy dishes, a conventional clock, and glass jars with screw-top lids. The new gooseneck faucet and porcelain handles reinforce the vintage look. Ticking-stripe window shades bring a soft touch to the plain surroundings.**

The living room speaks of a time when farm families didn't need a lot of material goods. "I looked for pieces that were comforting and comfortable," Lisa says. "I wanted simple, usable things—nice things, but not necessarily costly." The child's dress on the wall is a reminder of Amish simplicity; Mark framed it as a present for Lisa. White or cream paint unifies mismatched furniture throughout the house, while accent pieces, such as the bench-turned-coffee-table, add a punch of color. The screen door, contributed by friends, shuts with a satisfying country "whap."

**ABOVE:** The big blue hutch in the living room provides a focal point in a mostly pale color scheme and makes a perfect place to store extra blankets. **OPPOSITE:** Mark and Lisa's bedroom adjoins the living room through French doors. A trip to a nearby auction netted the bed and dresser for their room. "I got both for $80," Lisa says. "The two pieces had nice old off-white paint, and even though the bedroom wasn't quite done when I bought the pieces, I knew they would be perfect for it." Shutters substitute for curtains at the windows.

## weekend furnishing

By putting together classic farmhouse pieces in fresh ways, you can quickly and inexpensively furnish a home for easy weekend living. Here are a few must-haves.

• Painted wood furnishings, from chairs to old oak dressers and cupboards. Mix pieces in different colors for variety.

• Easy-care textiles in imperfect condition, such as old crib quilts and hooked or rag rugs. Display them on the wall unframed, or use them as table runners.

• Old benches to use everywhere: as a coffee table, for extra seating, or as a side table in the bedroom or bath.

• Baskets, both wire and wicker, that can be used for decoration and storage.

• Tools, such as ladders and rakes, that can be used for display.

**OPPOSITE ABOVE:** Mark, Lisa, and their children shuck corn. **OPPOSITE BELOW:** Planks saved from remodeling the McCormicks' "weekday" house top this trestle dining table. **ABOVE:** Lucy McCormick began collecting pastel-glazed flowerpots while toddling along with her parents at flea markets. She displays her collection on a ladder from a junk shop. A whitewashed oak bed, a wedding present stored away in the McCormicks' barn, went into the children's bedroom.

## design strategies

The qualities of simplicity, beauty, and utility have long embodied American country style. As country moves into a new century, those qualities still count—they're just interpreted in new ways that reflect contemporary demands for more space, less clutter, and an updated blend of form and function. Modern country is as true blue as it has ever been, with fresh twists.

**New country colors,** such as celadon and khaki, are inspired by nature and function as neutrals, working with almost any color scheme. Combined with coffee, cream, and white, they complement old-patina woods. Lighter versions of colors, such as pale lilac and the most translucent of blues, open up a room and give it more visual space.

**Furnishings are easy** to live with and sized for today's homes. New pieces combine easily with antiques, especially since many furnishings being produced today are modeled on country classics, such as wingback chairs or hexagonal tables. Upholstered with fresh fabrics, today's soft furnishings replace the dark, heavy colors and textures of yesterday's pieces with brighter materials that are versatile and easy to maintain.

**Familiar faces** are always welcome, but they may take on a new function. An antique blanket chest, for instance, may now store mix-and-match sheets and linens in fresh colors. Or an alpaca throw draped over a sofa may replace a handmade quilt, providing a more contemporary take on country's signature comfort.

### space savers

**BELOW: A long, narrow console table takes up little space and fits into almost any room of the house. Contemporary sculptural pottery, which assumes the place of honor given to milk glass or stoneware in the past, keeps the handmade touch in the home. RIGHT: Drawers extend this table's opportunities for storage, so that it works as well in a dining room for flatware and table linens as it does here for pillows and blankets. Such pieces are streamlined to suit today's smaller spaces.**

## simple abundance

**TOP LEFT:** Solid-colored linen upholstery, a fresh alternative to homespun checks and plaids, enhances the clean lines of this wood-frame sofa. **TOP RIGHT:** Molded plastic chairs express the same respect for simplicity as an antique pine harvest table, here freshened with a coat of white paint. A sleek new pitcher and bowl update country's classic blue-and-white color scheme. **RIGHT:** A reproduction four-poster epitomizes Shaker simplicity. Tailored bedding and a light color scheme make the room feel modern.

## a fresh approach

**LEFT:** A reproduction crookneck lamp offers clean line and form, and it directs light wherever you want it. **RIGHT:** Weathered stools can serve as easels for art, tables for chairside or bedside, or kitchen-counter seating. The new "true blue" country mixes weathered woods with smoothly finished ones for a look that's fresh but anchored in the past.

**Handmade folk art** and fine crafts are still a hallmark of country, but now they've gone global, thanks to easy access via the Internet. Combine a hand-hammered American pewter plate with a hand-thrown pot from Mexico, or supplement vintage wooden bowls with those from Turkey or Indonesia. Collect new versions of traditional favorites, too; for example, replace classic (and hard-to-find) botanical prints with new black-and-white photographs of flowers.

### dual purpose

**BELOW:** Versatility is essential to the new true blue country. Reproduction sofa and gaming tables can be pushed against a wall for a buffet or moved into the room for homework or letter writing. Imported baskets in traditional and novel shapes can hold everything from wine bottles to magazines. An umbrella stand doubles as a vase for a massive arrangement of branches or garden flowers. Think flexibility and multifunction, and you have one aspect of modern country.

### form and function

**ABOVE LEFT: A** century-old pie safe started out with screens for ventilation; later, it was fitted with glass for storage. Today the piece shows off new china, but tomorrow it could be enlisted to hold a CD or DVD player. **ABOVE:** Books can convey the essence of new blue country, outfitting your house with objects that are both useful and beautiful. Leather, suede, and printed covers look and feel good, and what's between them feeds the mind.

## new traditions

**ABOVE:** A soft-to-the-touch pillow sports a pinking-shear edge, suggesting handmade modesty.
**RIGHT:** A chair of woven straw with a leather seat preserves country's classic wingback shape and a love of all things natural and richly textured. **BELOW:** This pitcher's heft nods to stoneware pitchers of earlier times. The shape is clean and streamlined, the color fresh.

## country's roots

**ABOVE:** Each piece in this room reflects faithfulness to country's heritage. The hexagonal table was inspired by tea tables of the 18th century, and a brushed-denim love seat with bronze nailhead trim updates the conventional wingback style. Natural rugs in sisal, straw, jute, or hemp take the place of braided or woven rugs, offering new textured options.

## updated classic

Tapered legs and 18th-century styling combine with a pale blue woven check to give this traditional settee a modern country look. Its casters and diminutive size make it easy to move from spot to spot, or from room to room; it could provide extra seating in a dining room, for example. The settee characterizes the multipurpose appeal of modern country furnishings.

In the language of decorating, cottage style is the equivalent of your great-aunt's lace handkerchief. Pretty and practical, the style also awakens the senses with eye-pleasing lace trims, the fragrance of candles and sweet-smelling soaps, and wide rocking chairs that welcome body and soul. Classic cottages may sit seaside, decorated with shells and sailboats. Sometimes they're found on the edge of town, covered with vines and flowers and filled with vintage spreads and wicker settees. The style, though, can surface anywhere; it's the attitude that makes a house a cottage. Today's cottage style often incorporates a soft palette of greens, blues, yellows, and shades of lilac; it may rise to a brighter standard with crisp colors

## cottage

gathered from natural surroundings. Florals are everywhere, in wallpapers, fabrics, and dainty embroidered napkins. Glassware sparkles, whether it's clear or tinged with color. And furnishings are dressed in slipcovers, vintage-style upholstery, and layers of weathered paint. Cottage is serviceable, too, with handy tables, sturdy old beds from the family attic, and bare floors with throw rugs that are easy to sweep and shake out. Think flea markets, fresh flowers, vintage patterns, and a bit of romance, and you've defined today's expression of cottage country. Above all, it's light and airy, fresh and fun, and completely, unequivocally original.

# by the sea

Judy and Jeff Naftulin had been renting houses on Martha's Vineyard for more than eight years before deciding to build their own. Then one day they were out driving and saw it: the dream cottage they had been looking for, with a "for sale" sign in front. They weren't ready to leave the house they had just finished decorating, but they knew that if they didn't snap up this waterfront, weathered-gray-shingled beauty with spectacular views, then someone else would be living their dream. So they made a plan to buy the cottage and keep it as a rental until the day they were ready to move in.

Furnishing to lease meant thinking about the present as well as the future. Judy, an interior design consultant and former antiques shop owner, would do the job herself and try to keep expenses to a minimum. Vacationers require comfortable fabrics and furniture that are hard-wearing enough to survive rental after rental. And they deserve colors, patterns, and accessories that are welcoming and timeless, not trendy. The solution? Keep it simple. Judy painted rough plank walls white, left the pine floors bare, and dressed windows minimally to preserve ocean views. For a color palette, she lifted a scheme of deep blues, foamy whites, and natural tones from the surrounding seascape.

OPPOSITE: **Stylish yet practical, the 1930s metal stacking chairs pull up to a weathered chestnut table, where guests can gather for lunch. The rush-seat rocker is American; the painting is a copy of a Cezanne landscape. RIGHT: Judy Naftulin reads by the beach. FAR RIGHT: The weathered-gray shingle cottage features a roomy porch ideal for taking in the view and dining alfresco in warmer months. Gardening is kept to a few window boxes to preserve the site's natural grasses, sand dunes, and the occasional wildflower.**

**BELOW LEFT:** Beadboard cabinets paired with rows of drawers below create the effect of a country kitchen cupboard. Practical laminate flooring is impervious to wet feet. **BELOW RIGHT:** In the living room, an antique lace coverlet and a long bolster covered in old ticking embellish a cozy window seat. Cobalt blue glass bottles purchased at antiques fairs line up on a shelf above the windows. **OPPOSITE:** A collection of blue-and-white china illustrates how to create a focal point by using similar objects united by a common color. Vintage tablecloths tied like scarves around the easy chairs add a jaunty touch.

**For furnishings and accessories,** Judy selected from her own inventory and shopped favorite sources for fabrics. She slipcovered an old couch in a romantic blue-and-white floral print found at a fabric outlet and covered two easy chairs in white, washable cotton. Old wood and wicker furniture works as side tables, but for a coffee table she bought a new sisal piece sturdy enough to prop up tired feet.

**Collections on display** around the house add personality. Unframed paintings on canvas, sea fans, and old photographs of the area celebrate the cottage's seaside location. Judy saw her largest challenge in the space between the fireplace mantel and the living room's high, vaulted ceiling. She couldn't find just the right painting, so she decided to hang blue-and-white china. "I bought plates everywhere I went," she says, laughing at her own excess. More than 40 plates later, she had a display as dramatic as the view at high tide.

## on display

Antiques give rooms instant character. Here are some ideas from Judy Naftulin.

• Blue-and-white transferware plates of all sizes, shapes, and patterns offer a three-dimensional alternative to paintings or prints when you need to fill a large wall space.

• Look for vintage silver trophy cups to use as vases. Collect bowls in all sizes to hold everything from fruit to souvenir photographs.

• Create themed groupings: Here, treasures from the sea anchor a photograph of a beach cottage (actually, the Naftulins' cottage as it looked in the 1930s).

• Hang functional items so they're both decorative and practical. Guests can use Judy's collection of raffia bags to carry groceries from the market or beach essentials such as sunglasses and books.

ABOVE: The windows in the cozy upstairs sleeping niche have hinged interior screens that can be closed to keep out insects or thrown open to welcome ocean breezes. "Ready-to-wear" cafe curtains that might ordinarily hang above a kitchen sink are inexpensive, washable, and suitably casual. Walls, curtains, bed linens and wicker furniture are layered white-on-white to lull vacationers with dreamy comfort. OPPOSITE: A thin white cutwork valance filters light into a hazy sunshine comfortable for napping. White-enameled pitchers are useful throughout the cottage as vases or for serving iced tea.

# souvenirs & keepsakes

A mere four blocks from the Pacific Ocean, the Laguna Beach, California, home of Rich and Molly English sits on a slight slope. It's high enough to overlook the buildings separating it from the ocean waves, allowing its open French doors to capture the fresh sea breezes. That exceptional view attracted the Englishes to this house, nudging them from a decade of living in Berkeley. "I grew up in Southern California," Molly says. "We always talked about going back to the ocean. It was just a matter of finding the right house."

**When the Englishes** moved, they brought with them the collection of furnishings and souvenirs that inspired Molly's Camps and Cottages store in the Bay Area years ago. The collectibles are an easy fit in this new home, which was painted by previous owners in sun-soaked shades of green, blue, yellow, and red. The colors highlight the couple's favorite treasures: Antique hotel silver gleams and California plein-air paintings show to advantage against apple green walls; vibrant college pennants and vintage pillows create a warm and cozy look in buttercup yellow rooms.

**Built in 1939** as a second home, the structure originally had only four rooms. Successive owners added a family room, expanded patio area, back bedroom, and bath. Molly and Rich added their own changes, converting space off the back of the house into a master bedroom that opens through French doors onto a brick terrace. continued on page 60

OPPOSITE: **Hickory chairs and a late-1800s harvest table offer informal seating in the dining room. The table is set with Johnson Brothers Rose Chintz pattern china, Molly's childhood favorite. The garden trug on the shelves holds silverware.** RIGHT: **Loose arrangements of freshly picked flowers bring more color.** FAR RIGHT: **Hannah, one of the couple's two dogs, curls up by the front door, where a vintage advertising illustration adorns the wall. Embroidered turn-of-the-century pillows add vibrant hues. The bench, fashioned from old-growth redwood, was made by Steve Reed, a cabinetmaker in Berkeley.**

A mix of period pieces and regional art stamps the living room with the mark of cottage style. The chairs, dating from the 1930s, are covered with new fabric reminiscent of their early days. Steve Reed of Berkeley made the wooden table, a piece that can be used indoors or out. He also crafted the red cupboard, finishing it with 33 coats of paint. Over the cupboard hangs a California plein-air painting by 1920s artist Franklin Pebbles. The 1930s chandelier is one of the Englishes' favorite vintage items. An Adirondack mirror made of twigs and shells adds a natural camp-style touch to the mix.

Green custom-built shelves in the dining room provide a colorful backdrop for an extensive collection of imprinted commercial silver once used in hotels and on airlines and steamships. Such pieces are sought after at antiques fairs and flea markets because they blend beauty, history, and function.

**BELOW:** Molly English furnished the brick patio with vintage pieces. French doors connect the patio to the bedroom, extending the indoor-outdoor quality of the home. **OPPOSITE:** The Englishes replaced an office/wine cellar in the original garage with the master bedroom and sanded and stained the floor of old pine boards. The closets flanking the bed feature beadboard and white-painted trim with red insets. The traditional feather-star pattern of the new quilt blends with geometrics in the pillows, rug, and blanket. World War II Swiss Army baskets, once used to carry food to the troops, serve as extra storage above the closets.

The Englishes have filled the house with elements common to cottage-style decorating—painted furniture, rattan and wicker, baskets, folk art, and lots of small tables and benches that work in every room. Elements of the garden come inside, too, through bouquets of fresh flowers. "We don't have curtains because so many flowers grow up around the house that people can't simply walk by and peek in a window," Molly says. But the most distinctive element of the couple's new home is surely the unusual mix of treasures they've collected from journeys near and far, from folding camp stools to trophy cups, life savers, and handmade rawhide lampshades. "It's surprising," Molly says. "We've been holding onto these things for a long time, and they all seem to fit right in."

Cottage-style personality comes across in keepsakes such as souvenirs—those inexpensive items you pick up while traveling, to hold memories of favorite places. Here are a few of the Englishes' favorite finds.

• Hotel silver knives and forks, such as the set of 10 place settings Molly bought for $1. "It's from the La Quinta Hotel, a great old place in Palm Springs," she says. "I found the set at an old salvage store. It's the best deal I ever made."

• Turn-of-the-century beacon blankets and embroidered pillows from different states, often featuring landmarks, such as Mount Rushmore.

• Pennant quilts. The couple has two brightening the twin beds in the guest room. Both are early 20th century; one features schools from the East and Midwest, the other is made of banners from California colleges.

**BELOW:** A collection of early 20th-century plein-air landscape paintings turns a corner into an art gallery. A cushion made from a rag rug softens the stick wicker chair; a fold-up camp stool serves as a makeshift table. The cupboard houses a CD player and tape deck. **OPPOSITE BOTTOM LEFT:** A beaded horseshoe found in Northern California is one of Molly's most treasured collectibles. **OPPOSITE TOP RIGHT:** Twin beds in the guest room display two favorite finds: quilts made from wool-and-felt pennants handstitched in the early 1900s. **OPPOSITE BOTTOM RIGHT AND BELOW:** Trophy cups serve as flower vases throughout the house.

# relaxed &
# romantic

Sue Balmforth loves to surround herself with fresh flowers, but she's quick to point out that there are times when a single bloom has as much impact as a whole bouquet. "Romantic doesn't mean overdone," says the owner of Bountiful, an antiques store and growing enterprise in Venice, California. "In some rooms, romantic means simple and easy." That relaxed attitude is evident throughout this Malibu beach house, where a pine farm table and a crystal chandelier are equally at home.

Sue began developing her signature style with her first antique purchase: an 1870s cowboy dresser she bought when she was 13 years old. Years later, when she moved from Bountiful, Utah, to Los Angeles, she took a job traveling with The Pointer Sisters. Soon she was spending days on the road antiquing with Ruth Pointer. "She was my partner in crime," Sue says. "Wherever we went, the two of us went antiquing." In 1991, Sue decided to start an antiques business of her own. At first, she sold country pieces from her apartment and at a local flea market. Eager to find and sell "real" antiques, she flew to Orlando, rented an 18-foot truck, and shopped her way back home. "If I was excited about something, I bought it," she says. Now, in addition to her 12,000-square-foot antiques store, she also has a lighting workshop, a furniture restoration studio, an art gallery, frame shop, and a penchant for selling architectural fragments. continued on page 71

OPPOSITE: **A romantic cottage style relies on a mix of surprising and contrasting elements. In equal measures, textures are rough, like the surface of the vintage chair, and smooth, like the finish on the old pail. The palette is a playful blend of natural hues, including green, yellow, lilac, blue, and pink.** RIGHT: **Overlooking the beach at Malibu, this home has outdoor space for dining, where furniture remains outside to weather naturally in the sun and sea air.** FAR RIGHT: **Flowers offer special inspiration to cottage decorating, with intense hues of purplish pinks and raspberry making their way indoors.**

Mismatched elements and unanticipated pairings create elegance in the dining room. Lace contrasts nicely with worn painted chairs that have been well waxed for a subtle sheen. Candlesticks in a variety of shapes and sizes are all crystal, which unifies the variety of shapes and introduces a light, sparkling quality to the room. Sprays of flowers infuse the room with a natural feeling, and a wicker basket and love seat, borrowed from the outdoors, enhance the impression of a fresh garden setting. In the background, squares of ceiling tin frame a large mirror, which visually expands the room.

**OPPOSITE:** Fresh and spacious, the kitchen gathers up all the colors of the sea and transports them indoors. The sleek, functional appliances contrast with timeless country elements: a grooved ceiling reminiscent of beadboard, a one-time mercantile cabinet (now topped with marble and serving as an island), and a crisp cloth on the table. Farmhouse touches, such as the bare wood floor and blue chairs, add to the flavor of classic country. **ABOVE:** A vintage tablecloth sets off pretty pitchers and glasses. Unmatched painted chairs drawn up to the table lend a casual, welcoming feeling.

**OPPOSITE:** An old painted cupboard provides storage space for linens, books, or a TV and CD player. **BELOW LEFT:** Dressing beds in layers of fabric, from fine cutwork and lace cloths to antique bed linens, creates a rumpled yet romantic look. **BELOW RIGHT:** An antique bed that looks as though it could have come from Grandmother's attic imparts a touch of refinement to this bedroom. Bed lamps with handsewn shades by Penni Oliver hang at each side of the headboard for reading. Over the headboard, an old dresser mirror hangs as art. A painted occasional table is the right height for bedside duty.

Sue also designs her own lines of custom mirrors framed in ceiling tin or barn board, as well as lampshades and pillows fashioned from lace, tapestries, and vintage fabrics. For decorating her own home or those of her clients, she relies on favorite touches. She places loose arrangements of flowers throughout the house, enlisting ironstone pitchers as vases. Victorian floral paintings are framed in old barn wood or fluted Victorian trim molding. And she uses wicker furnishings indoors and out for a light, casual mood. The finishes, too, are easy and comfortable, with paint and rough textures mixed with smooth cottons and crystal candlesticks. Chandeliers, a personal favorite, are something of a hallmark for Sue, who has more than 100 hanging in her shop. "They are my greatest extravagance," she says. Like her easy and romantic mix of cottage elements, "they turn the country look into something special."

Chandeliers hanging in unusual or unexpected places—such as a bathroom, powder room, or dressing room—add a feeling of elegance and luxury. Gauzy curtains make a billowy backdrop for the whirlpool bath. Ornate garden urns hold potted plants for color and, more practically, plenty of fresh towels beside the bath.

## creating the bountiful look

To incorporate some of Sue Balmforth's signature elements of cottage decorating, try these simple techniques.

• Rely on painted pieces to warm a room. The cupboard, mirror, and door in the photo opposite lend a comfortable, vintage touch to this powder room.

• Introduce bits of ironwork. A metal-edged three-way mirror, iron-and-crystal chandelier, and wire basket all add pattern and function.

• Incorporate floral touches wherever you can. Whether through a fresh bouquet, a rug design, or floral painting on a headboard, flowers invite the outdoors inside with simple charm and beauty.

• Use fabric in ways that evoke romance. For example, allowing long draperies of lightweight fabric to puddle on bare wood floors suggests a generous luxuriousness.

# ocean colors

"Color makes me happy," says Cynthia O'Connor, a clothing accessories executive who delights in discovering new hues and color combinations. "I keep a bulletin board tacked full of color chips and fabric swatches that catch my attention," she says. "It's a handy way to see how you respond to them over time." Color was conspicuously absent, however, in the 1879 Victorian house she and her husband, Fuller, found just a block from the water's edge in Bay Head, New Jersey. Wrapped in a cloak of dark tones and wallpaper, it had nothing of the light, beachy feel that Cynthia had envisioned for a family weekend retreat.

Transforming the house with a fresh, airy color scheme was no problem for Cynthia. "I started by buying two paint-chip fans from the paint store, one to cut up and one to refer to," she says. Sunlight moving through the house provided her with a palette of whispery sky blues, seaweed greens, and frothy whites for the south-facing front rooms. For darker rooms at the back of the house, the color scheme took on deeper, more vivid tones. Outside, she painted the screen door a sunburst yellow. Weathered shingles were enlivened with shades of ocean blue and green. Both outside and in, she capped her ocean palette with bright white paint, using it on trim and furniture.

To achieve the casual look of cottage style, Cynthia mixes tables, chairs, and chests that have scuffed painted surfaces with freshly painted furniture. Sofas and armchairs continued on page 84

OPPOSITE: White painted furniture appears in every room, tying the house together visually and giving it a cottage feeling. Cynthia O'Connor wanted the house to be comfortable yet formal enough to feel like a real home and not just a "crash pad." The curves of a Victorian-inspired arm chair show to advantage with new upholstery. RIGHT: Wicker and rocking chairs turn the porch of the house into a welcoming spot for relaxing. FAR RIGHT: A frosted glass vase standing on a milk glass dish becomes an inventive light source with the addition of a pillar candle.

The inviting color scheme of blues, greens, and whites in the living room appears to have been plucked from the sea. Pillows add an extra layer of comfort to the put-your-feet-up seating area, which centers on a simple plank coffee table. Large knitting baskets double as storage bins, holding magazines under the side tables. The sisal rug is a low-maintenance floor covering.

OPPOSITE: In the dining room, wallpaper provides a colorful backdrop for a disparate collection of American and Swedish furniture, united by the color of the paint. An ornate painted iron chandelier wears tailored shades and hangs from a ceiling washed with pale blue to evoke the sky. ABOVE: The buffet provides storage for dinnerware and table linens. Propping a tall, ornately framed mirror on the buffet strikes a casual note and enhances the room's light-filled feeling. The seat cushions on the metal chairs are covered with a companion to the fabric on the living room couch, helping to link the two rooms visually.

**OPPOSITE:** At the top of the stairs, a former "doggie gate" takes on the appearance of a garden fence with its new coat of white paint. **BELOW:** Layers of bedding—throws, comforters, spreads, shams, sheets, and pillows—in a medley of colors and textures add up to sink-in comfort. The beadboard paneling, rag rug, and weathered paint romance the past.

**BELOW LEFT:** A bedroom bureau with paint worn to the color of sand holds an arrangement of white accessories—vintage milk glass, an old lamp, and a salvaged mirror. **BELOW RIGHT:** The bedroom of 7-year-old daughter Virginia glows with yellow wallpaper, bright coral pink accents, and a vintage chenille spread. **OPPOSITE:** Using the same toile fabric on the chair, bedskirt, and pillow shams brings bed-and-breakfast formality to the cozy master suite, while bare floors, casual shirt-plaids, and practical venetian blinds freshen the mood and keep the room light and breezy.

upholstered in a mix of casual solid fabrics and dressier prints lend a genteel feel to the rooms. To prevent the look from becoming too coordinated, Cynthia piles on homey pillows and throws fashioned from the vintage fabrics she enthusiastically collects. Table and dresser tops are crowned with groupings of family photos and treasures ranging from inexpensive milk glass and gathered seashells to fine silver—all knit together by color or patina.

Cynthia's knack for adhering to a scheme delivers a mood that's both cozy and invigorating. "Being in this house is so wonderful and uplifting," says Cynthia. "I sit on the sofa and feel the breeze coming through the door—it gives me such a warm feeling."

## an eye for vintage

Cynthia O'Connor (below left) heeded the advice of her good friend, interior designer Ann Fox (below right) and began to collect in bulk the vintage fabric she loves: 1940s, '50s, and '60s kitchen tablecloths and cocktail napkins, chenille bedspreads, hand towels, and pillowcases. Her advice:

• Collect as much as you can, even stained or torn pieces. A ready supply will give you the freedom to cut pieces up to make pillows or throws or to cover seat cushions.

• Old curtains can be an excellent source of fabric for reupholstering benches or chairs.

• Use piping to trim the edges of cushions or to define the shapes of upholstered pieces. The piping dresses up the piece and gives it crispness.

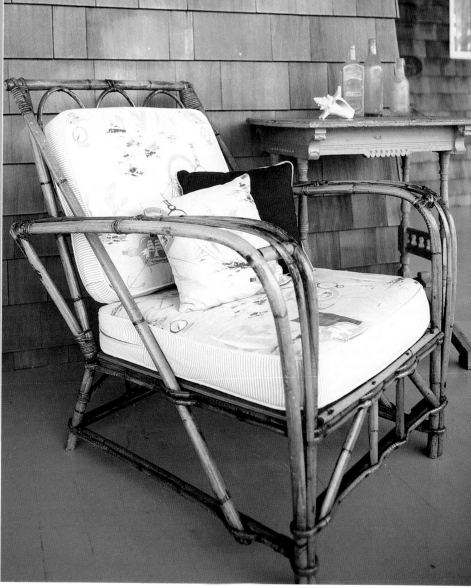

# cottage
## design strategies

Cottage-style decorating promises a simpler life—a life in which a little wear and tear is instantly excused and china plates and cups were never meant to match. Inspired by nature, cottage decorating is a swirl of floral chintzes and opalescent buttons. It's a style in which fabric scraps are saved and used, and leftover bits of wallpaper are put in a basket instead of on the wall.

**Like flowers** in the garden, cottage colors mix naturally, making it simple to coordinate paint, wallpaper, and fabric. In fact, it's hard to go wrong with a cottage palette, in which white provides an easy backdrop for just about any hue you could choose. For color schemes, look to nature: the blue of a robin's egg, the green of a lamb's-ear leaf, the yellow of butter, and the coral of a conch shell.

**Furnishings are as easy** as the colors; if a piece doesn't fit, just paint it, upholster it, or throw a slipcover over it, and you're done. With today's selection of nostalgic fabrics, you can find a pattern that will take you right back to your grandmother's dresses; add a box pleat or a lace edging and you've created instant cottage style.

### florals and stripes
**BELOW:** With cottage style, you can be fearless in mixing and matching fabrics, such as vintage florals and ticking stripes. Soft ruffles and tailored button closures add an extra bit of sweet detail. **RIGHT:** Fresh as the outdoors, cottage gains much of its inspiration from the garden. In this case, wicker furniture and a painted table could move indoors or out for tea in the garden or the living room. A mix of pillows and throws softens wicker seating with make-do upholstery.

## worn and weathered

**ABOVE: A** cottage offers a place to relax and enjoy the perfection of imperfection. This pillow's floral fabric pretties up the wicker chair's weathering paint, a contrast for which cottage style is famous. **BELOW:** Garden accents brought indoors lend an instant feeling of cottage to any setting. Abundant lilac blossoms, loosely arranged in a painted pail, are every bit as informal as a set of vintage glasses.

## fresh air

**ABOVE: A** light, fresh attitude unifies unrelated fabrics and patterns—as does a bit of whimsy. A pineapple chandelier sheds light on a cozy grouping that enlists a cast-off as a coffee table and layers rug upon rug for extra comfort. Wicker pieces stand ready to be moved outside on a sunny day.

## charm school

**ABOVE: D**ecorating in the cottage style offers an abundance of opportunities to create dainty still lifes of objects you enjoy. A new mirror framed in old pressed-tin ceiling tiles can simply rest on a cupboard or dresser to reflect light and whatever interesting bottles, flowers, or other collectibles you place in front of it. Give a flea market lamp a cottage look by covering the shade with a scrap of vintage floral fabric.

The fun of cottage decorating lies in the details—all the collectibles that will fill your house with memories. Look for flower prints with painted frames, crystal candlesticks, and fancy drawer pulls; embroidered cloths that can be turned into little bags or cushions; and gifts from nature, such as rose petals or mother-of-pearl buttons. If in doubt, don't skimp on the florals or fringe, and abandon all but the things you love.

### outdoor inspiration

**RIGHT:** Reminiscent of an earlier time, this all-vintage look features an easy mix that works because of the soft colors. From stemware to spoons, nothing needs to match. Look for pressed glass in pale colors and different designs, vintage tablecloths, and contrasting napkins. For a vase, any old pitcher will do. **BELOW:** Peeling paint and a weathered urn give instant age to fresh floral fabrics and a loose arrangement of flowers. Everything is secondhand; similar items are easy to find at thrift stores or yard sales. To showcase each piece, keep displays simple and uncluttered.

### quick cover-up

**ABOVE:** Quintessentially cottage, slipcovers can disguise anything, even a secondhand straightback chair. This loose slipcover is edged with a bit of piping, a dressmaker's detail that gives it a mark of distinction. The barely gathered skirt lends an extra flounce. For a touch of romance, a lace-edged tablecloth tumbles almost to the floor.

## sweetness and light

**ABOVE:** Outfitted with light bulbs or candles, chandeliers have a dressed-for-the-party look that adds sparkle to any room. **BELOW:** Thanks to its shape, color, and upholstery, this thrift store chair is as sweet and likable as a little girl's dress. The tiny rosebuds blend well with the floral wallpaper; a pillow made from an old throw boasts a row of fringe and a flower all its own.

## mixing it up

**ABOVE:** Extravagant detail makes this cabinet majestic; a wash of white paint makes it cottage. Converted to a bathroom vanity, it offers ample space for colored bottles and a vintage candelabra. **LEFT:** Cottage style makes room for the most unexpected of collections, such as baseballs displayed with flowers and a seltzer bottle. **BELOW:** Cushions covered in easy-care fabric soften a wicker settee.

In the history of country decorating, the word "rustic" has conjured up a host of mental pictures. It conveys a lakeside cabin where a canoe and oars rest near the screen door; a row of rough hickory rockers with ticking-striped pillows lined up on a porch overlooking an open meadow; rough-hewn baskets and ironware made in a time when household goods were crafted by hand. No doubt, all such images are quintessentially rustic, featuring furnishings and accessories characterized by their instant patina and weathered, well-used character. So what makes rustic new? More light. More space. And smart solutions. Rustic still means dark colors, earthenware containers, iron and leather, copper and wood. But today it's

# rustic

rearranged, replicated, and refreshed to make homes more livable. Newly defined, rustic is carefully edited, with fewer dust catchers and more functional pieces. It's peaceful and eclectic, mixing European with American regional antiques, and showcasing natural surfaces and pioneering spirit. In short, rustic is still timber, homespun fabrics, and galvanized tin, but it's also serviceable, sleek, and slightly sophisticated. It's rooted in the most honored traditions of country, embracing the Texas ranch house, the Indiana farmstead, and the New England saltbox. It's also the place where the shoes come off, the preserves are put up, and the heart and soul find constant comfort.

# log cabin revival

Building a new house can be daunting enough, but rebuilding an old house, with no floor plan to work from, takes a bit of creative genius and a crystal-clear vision. Terry and Brenda Blackburn have both: The proof is in their farm home, a successful blend of an 1849 log house and new construction. The project began in Kentucky, where the couple found an abandoned log house and had it disassembled, numbered, and transported to their five-acre property in Indiana. Then they began reassembling the pieces. "Every day was a challenge," Brenda says. "We had taken photographs, but then we lost them." After some initial log-raising weekends, when friends and family helped to set the first logs, the Blackburns and Terry's father, Claud, worked daily for two years rebuilding the two-room house from scratch. Along the way, they heaved 24-foot logs into position, acquired a crash course in old-fashioned chinking techniques, and outfitted the house for the 21st century with a bathroom, a kitchen, a second-floor loft, front and back porches, and a utility room.

To blend the new construction with the original log structure, the Blackburns used cedar siding and quarter-sawn oak that weathered almost immediately. Inside, they also left the logs untreated, instantly achieving an aged effect. Installing pine and poplar floors and keeping furnishings and accessories to a minimum underscored the continued on page 98

OPPOSITE: **Measuring 18x22 feet, the kitchen resembles the old-fashioned farm kitchen of Brenda Blackburn's dreams. The old cast-iron sink with its original faucets came from a friend. Terry built the red cupboard from pine board, while a local blacksmith hand-forged the hinges. A local artisan made the tin chandelier, based on a photograph Brenda clipped from a magazine; Brenda added a coat of white paint. The table and chairs came from a flea market and antiques dealer.** RIGHT: **An oak-splint basket made by Trevle Wood rests on a chair on the front porch.** FAR RIGHT: **Gourds hang on a fence built from old fence posts and barn boards.**

**OPPOSITE:** Using 6-inch-wide pine boards for the flooring gives instant age to the kitchen. The antique blue-gray table is portable enough to be moved around the kitchen for breadmaking and extra work space. The stove, marked with a patent date of 1926, was purchased from a man who had moved it from California after using it for years. "Even the thermostat still works," Brenda says. **BELOW:** Cauliflower heads make a pleasing temporary arrangement in a 3-foot-long bread bowl. In other seasons, the bowl holds fruit, the harvest of the day, or branches of rose hips.

BELOW: Simple and serene, the bathroom combines items that Brenda collected long before she knew where she would use them. She decorated the floor's new pine boards with a stencil design borrowed from a friend. The claw-foot tub cost $40 at a garage sale; it was in good condition and only needed reglazing. A handmade pine shelf holds towels, while an antique wall-hung cabinet provides additional storage. OPPOSITE: The front entry marks the division of the cabin's original two rooms. A sign honors the dates of the cabin's first and second construction.

primitive look. The couple opted not to hang curtains so they could enjoy the country view. "When we look out one window, we can see the creek," Brenda says. "When we look out the other, we can see the woods."

The sparse look of the home was part of the plan from the beginning. "We only brought things to this house that we knew we would use," Brenda says. She credits Terry for his guidance. When she was ready to hang baskets on a wall one day, for example, Terry discouraged her. "We love the look of the logs," he said. "Let's just keep it simple." The result is a home that is comfortable, functional, and true to its country roots. "I collected a lot of things for the house, not knowing where I'd put them," Brenda said. By choosing only the things she loved—and not too many of them—everything fit, just like the puzzle pieces of the log home.

1849·BACK CREEK CABIN·1997

The second floor of the house measures 18x36 feet—spacious enough to house two beds in an open loft area. The 19th-century rope bed came from a friend who also owned a log cabin. Brenda stitched the coverlet and pillowcases from homespun blue plaid fabric; a piece of vintage linen drapes over the footboard. Additional antique furnishings with their original finishes extend the farmhouse feel to the upstairs.

ABOVE: **The dining room occupies one of the cabin's two original rooms. The Blackburns' oldest son made the table, which measures almost 10 feet long, as a gift from all the couple's children. The bench came from a Mennonite meeting house. Brenda purchased the chairs unfinished and gave them a wash of green-black paint. A local artisan made the tin chandelier; a collection of old wooden bowls adorns the wall.**

ABOVE: To build the fireplace, the Blackburns salvaged stones from a local building that was being razed. The mantel was cut from one of the beams in the original log cabin. Traditional fabrics cover a new sofa and chairs; the workbench behind the sofa came from an Indiana antiques shop. For the floor, the couple collected old poplar boards and had them planed down to resemble those in an old log home.

OPPOSITE: **A pie safe with its original bittersweet-color paint has weak hinges, so Brenda uses it to store items she doesn't need very often. To lend a rustic look to the staircase wall, the Blackburns built it from tongue-and-groove pine siding. A new miniature quilt adds color as a wall hanging.** ABOVE: **A dry sink with peeling paint came from a local antiques dealer; Terry's brother Jim made the small house next to the oak-splint basket. Above the dry sink, the frame of an old tray turned on its side serves as a shelf for a vintage checkerboard and bowls.**

A dresser at the top of the stairs is draped with a linen-wool runner. A tin sewing box still held old needles and thread when Brenda bought it. A framed picture of Brenda and her sister hangs over the dresser. OPPOSITE, CLOCKWISE FROM TOP RIGHT: The Blackburns bought the tin candle sconce from an antiques store in Indiana long before they constructed their log house. Brenda snaps green beans on the porch. A basket holds pieces of homespun fabric.

# modern saltbox

In Nederland, Texas, most people build low-maintenance, modern houses designed to survive the region's hurricanes and hot, humid weather. Betty and James Stansbury, however, wanted something different: a New England-style saltbox that would suit their collection of country antiques. Amassed over years of antiquing in Massachusetts and Connecticut, the blanket chests, Windsor chairs, and stoneware jugs seemed to demand a setting more sympathetic than the usual brick house with aluminum windows. After studying country magazines and books of house plans, the couple eventually decided to blend two mail-order house plans and make some alterations to create their dream home. "I knew what we would need to be comfortable," Betty says. "Just two bedrooms and a really large place to have meals because we entertain a lot. Where the original plan had a dining room and family room, we combined it into a large keeping room. And a back hall became a pantry for us that's always full."

The next steps were to clear the 1½ acres of land for the house and to find someone to build it. To make sure the house turned out the way they wanted it, James acted as general contractor, and the Stansburys did all of the finish work themselves. James made interior paneling from barn siding, while Betty painted the wide plank floor in the kitchen. Exemplifying their eye for detail and authenticity, Betty painted the floor three times, first with a layer of black, then white,

OPPOSITE: **Treenware lines a mantel that fits Betty Stansbury's primitive-style decorating scheme. The couple found the baskets at flea markets. The blue settle dates to the late 1700s. James used barn siding, salvaged doors, and plank floors and ceilings to create interiors with colonial character. He built the extra-deep, extra-wide fireplaces to 18th-century specifications.** RIGHT AND FAR RIGHT: **To house their collection of country antiques, Betty and James Stansbury chose the classic saltbox design; the name refers to the steep roof profile, which recalls boxes used for storing salt. The couple combined two mail-order house plans to create the blueprint for the house.**

then mustard, with no sealers in between. Before long, scuffing from natural wear and tear revealed the alternate colors below and gave the kitchen a well-worn look almost instantly. "The older and rougher something looks, the better for this new house," James says. "If it was too perfect, we'd rip it out and start over."

Imperfections characterize the furnishings too. Wood pieces remain as close as possible to their original state, highlighted by accessories chosen for their handmade quality. Reproductions blend seamlessly with the antiques, and Betty dresses the windows simply, fastening fabric to the woodwork with rosehead nails or wrought-iron scroll hooks. Although the house doesn't look like any other in Nederland, Texas, it is the perfect place for the Stansburys to showcase their collection of New England country classics.

## instant age

With a clear vision of the look they wanted to achieve, the Stansburys incorporated a number of aging techniques in building and decorating their home. "We didn't try to make the door fit the frame," says James. "We would make the frame crooked to fit the old door." Here are a few ideas to borrow.

• Use historic paint colors and milk paints to achieve authenticity. Also look at period paintings for clues to appropriate fabrics.

• Incorporate salvaged paneling, doors, and ceilings whenever possible. You'll need to have antique barnwood replaned and fumigated before you use it.

• Choose reproduction double-hung windows with 8-over-12 panes.

• Look for reproduction lighting fixtures with aged finishes of iron or copper.

OPPOSITE: The kitchen combines Shaker simplicity with modern efficiency. James built the cabinets himself, using three boards for each door and purposely making the slats different widths to look authentic. For the walls, Betty applied a thick coat of premixed joint compound over drywall to simulate plaster. Stoneware jars and jugs, found mainly at East Coast flea markets, are both decorative and functional. The sawbuck table and hanging lantern on the left are antique, but the fixture over the sink is new. ABOVE: The couple's granddaughter likes to nap on the reproduction rope bed, which is blanketed with a linen center-seam coverlet. A chest from the early 1800s serves as a bedside table. Brown plaid fabric secured with rosehead nails dresses the window.

By adjusting the floor plan, the Stansburys opened up the keeping room to make their period-inspired space more livable. The furnishings evoke New England character without slavishly reproducing an 18th-century interior. An upholstered Woodstock chair, with a tall back and sides to block drafts, and a new Queen-Anne-style sofa anchor a thoroughly modern conversational grouping. The blue chest, bearing its original paint, serves as a coffee table. Curtains throughout the house soften the architecture without blocking light. In this room, hand-pleated fabric drapes over simple iron hooks. Other iron hooks hold baskets in keeping with the period style.

# home to heritage

When Linda Gray inherited the Texas homestead her family settled four generations ago, she had more memories than hope for the ramshackle house on a creek bottom. The tiny two-bedroom structure, built in 1888 by her great-grandparents, had served over the years as a bunkhouse and barn. "I remember going upstairs as a little girl and seeing hay stacked from floor to ceiling in the bedrooms," says Linda, who didn't revisit the house again until she was a teenager in the early 1970s. Relieved at the sight of indoor plumbing, she took a long, loving look at the ranch house's original wide plank floorboards, worn stenciled walls, and deep, shady porches. She urged her mother to renovate the house as a weekend home. Linda's parents put on a new roof and patched it up just enough to give their family more than 25 years of weekend fun on the ranch. But time had been less than kind to the structure. When Linda took ownership of the property, windows leaked and beams were giving way. And the house had no living room and a too-cramped kitchen.

The solution Linda and her husband, Rod, devised was to grow the house along with their family. Rather than knocking down walls, they would keep the original structure intact as a bedroom wing and add an open-plan kitchen/dining/living space. They moved the house 400 yards onto a

OPPOSITE: **In the dining area, the family gathers at an old European farmhouse table and sits on spindle-back chairs that came from a stick-to-your-ribs Texas restaurant. Apples turn an old chicken-feed trough into a rustic centerpiece.** RIGHT: **The original late-19th-century Texas homestead was relocated 400 yards to a shady site under aging oaks, then tripled in size with the addition of this new wing. Inside, the wing's layout is modern, but outside, the tin-roofed structure stays true to the old style with deep porches and pitched dormer windows.**

new foundation and built the new wing in the same footprint, including 12-foot-deep porches. A concrete-floored mud hall connects the buildings. Linda furnished the house with a mix of heirlooms and country furniture purchased at Round Top, the local blockbuster antiques fair. Houston interior designer Ginger Barber helped her meld the new wing with the old, deciding on a quiet palette of saddle-leather brown, taupes, and faded forest greens. Color is more plentiful in the bedrooms, found on patchwork quilts and plank walls untouched since 1906, when Linda's great-grandparents hired an itinerant artist to paint murals and stencils. Never covered, never restored, and rained on when there was no roof, the decorative painting survives, soaked into the warm patina of the wood grain. If the old walls could speak, they might well praise this new generation's make-do approach to history, tradition, and everyday practicality.

ABOVE: **A muted palette of soft neutrals gives the new addition its lived-in look, while a Persian carpet, smoothly tailored leather chairs, and a tufted, nailhead-trimmed ottoman contribute an air of gentility. The room has central-air conditioning for hot Texas summers, but owes its genuinely breezy mood to ceiling fans and walls of windows and doors.** OPPOSITE: **The old homestead connects to the new wing via this mud hall, where a bright folk painting contrasts with the browns of rustic furniture and baskets purchased at local fairs and shops. Overhead light comes from hanging vintage brass domes, whose spare design appears both country and modern. The powder room door, fitted with frosted glass and a mail slot, once hung in a London office.**

This mural, painted in 1906, is one of a pair on opposing walls in the dog run, which was originally the main living space of the old house. The stenciled frame is new. OPPOSITE: The dog run was both entryway and living room in the old house, with bedrooms branching off of it. Now one end leads to the mud hall, which connects the old house to the new wing. Furnished with a daybed and wicker chair, it serves as a refuge for company when lots of guests visit for the weekend.

## gathering spaces

Linda's great-grandparents built their house around a long corridor to let breezes flow through, but the Gray family's biggest concern today is crowd control. Here are some of their space-making ideas.

• A game table in the living room provides a place to play dominoes as well as to have meals. For a small group, the table is more intimate than the big dining table, and for large crowds, it supplies overflow seating.

• A bump-out in the kitchen holds a trestle table that doubles as a work station.

• Positioning an old work table in the kitchen defines the preparation area and offers the flexibility that a permanent island could not. With two sinks, commercial appliances, and ample storage space, the room is as hardworking as country kitchens of the past, but with a lot more convenience.

The original back porch, furnished with antique wicker of the period, was screened in to keep mosquitoes at bay in warm weather. The family gathers here in the evening before dinner when the northern exposure is most scenic. "It's a feel-good place to look toward the golden hours," says Linda.

# rustic design strategies

The new frontier in rustic decorating is more than a mix of sticks and stone. It's a bounty of natural woods and wicker, leather and unbleached linen, heavy wool, and breathable cottons. This fresh, sophisticated interpretation of rustic style owes much to elegant 19th-century sporting lodges, whose sprawling spaces seem reborn in today's big-as-the-outdoors great-rooms.

**More and more windows** are piercing log and barn-board walls that were originally sealed to hold heat in winter and keep interiors cool in summer. Airy rattan replaces thick slat frames on furniture, while dark beams and peeling bark surfaces have given way to smoother new woods in lighter, honey-hued, or cherry finishes. Natural fabrics such as linen, burlap, hemp, and cotton replace the somber colors and patterns of traditional upholstery, and windows sport airy sheers or are left unadorned. Likewise, chopped-up floor plans are replaced by open spaces designed to be clutter-free.

**Rustic style spans** oceans and time. English brass or Asian rattan and jute are welcome additions to woodsy Adirondack lodges and Kentucky cabins, while choices in furniture and accessories mix early Shaker, Country Chippendale, and 20th-century Arts and Crafts designs.

**Lodge furniture** is traditionally oversized to echo the largeness of a mountainscape and the strength of its frontiersmen. Proportions remain big and bold, but forms are no longer bulky. Lines are spare and clean, and upholstery tightly fitted in the

### smooth finishes
**BELOW: A streamlined cherry sideboard makes an elegant statement with its smooth-as-silk finish, Chippendale-style hardware, and gently tapered legs. RIGHT: The thin slats on this Early American-inspired love seat make the large-scaled piece seem airy. Though made of hardwoods, the piece conveys soft sentiment, with cabriole legs, curved arms, and a joined back for two.**

## a lighter look

**ABOVE:** Instead of the bulky, gnarled pieces of the past, new rustic furniture includes rattan with shapes inspired by vintage 1930s design. Unbleached linen upholsters the cushions, and white walls keep the woodsy look fresh and airy.
**RIGHT:** Subdivide large spaces with furniture arrangement. A cherry sideboard behind the love seat limits the seating area within the expanse of a great-room, for example. **BELOW:** Hand-thrown pottery that's both functional and collectible is the modern version of antique redware.

## updated lines

**ABOVE:** Borrowing from Shaker design, a sideboard with apothecary-style drawers offers storage with beauty; the American wing chair has been reproportioned with a sleeker profile. The country-French-inspired armoire is actually a modern entertainment center. **BELOW:** Traditional tartans and tattersall patterns have been updated in a more muted palette.

more aerodynamic style of vintage 1930s and 1940s furniture. In small rooms, fewer pieces suffice without sacrificing scale.

From the salt glazes on hand-thrown pottery to the dull gleam of brown leather, new rustic design favors a subtle shine over the weathered and matte surfaces of the past. Woods also add a new sophistication to this down-to-earth style. Grains are finer, surfaces smoother, and details expertly crafted, from complex joinery to sleekly tapered legs.

### unfussy accessories

RIGHT: **Black-and-white photographs are a staple of vintage cabin decorating. For a contemporary spin, surround old photos in white mats and plain frames.** FAR RIGHT: **Clear glass and white linens add freshness and light to rustic schemes, where simplicity reigns and materials are free of excess ornament.**

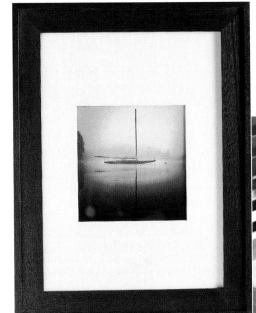

### dressed-up rustic

LEFT: **Give rustic country rooms a more formal feeling with classic architecture and traditionally styled Chippendale chairs crafted from warm, red cherry. Choose natural burlap for curtains and pale jute for the rug to enhance the lightened-up look. And whenever possible, make the most of views that underscore the connection to the great outdoors.**

## subtle sheen

**ABOVE:** Bring in a feeling of light with subtly reflective surfaces, such as the smooth-planed woods of a new cupboard and the glazes of hand-thrown pottery. **BELOW:** The leather on this sofa is a luxurious update on the traditional earth tones of rustic decorating. The form, however, is early Modern; straight contours and expert tailoring keep the large-scale sofa looking lean.

## contrasting textures

**ABOVE:** Polished wood frames the rough brick on an overscaled fireplace. Try layering sepia-toned photos on the mantel instead of wooden bowls. **RIGHT:** A picket fence cobbled together from odd boards makes a fitting backdrop for country flowers. **BELOW:** An old water pump with original blue paint serves as garden sculpture.

**What does a Navajo blanket** have in common with English blue-and-white china? Or a 1940s electric fan with a farmer's best straw hats? The connection is an intimate one, drawn by homeowners who mine history and global culture for the essence of country design. Whether in vignettes of cowboy collectibles or old French paperbacks, personal country is about boldly expressing your passions. Inspiration may come from anywhere—the regional culture, the surrounding landscape, or your own memories. A coastal retreat can emulate a seaborn yacht, a sun-drenched Tucson home Provençal dreams, or a Manhattan loft the joie de vivre of Paris. The look is fashionable and flexible, relying more on accessories than architecture. With the

# personal

turning seasons, fabrics change from floral cottons to wool plaids, and centerpieces from wildflowers to dried grasses. Souvenirs from recent travels mix with treasured family heirlooms and inexpensive flea market finds. Personal country rethinks castaway objects, adding a new drawer to a folding tray table for use as a desk, or draping vintage hand towels as cafe curtains. Collections may abound, but imagination and a strong sense of play are really the stars in each artful display. Like different actors bringing their life experiences to the same role, this seemingly eclectic style brings together strong personalities reflecting on time-honored country traditions.

# french
## connection

Several stories up from street level and the blare of horns and car alarms, Liz Dougherty Pierce and her husband, Michael, find calm in the open spaces of their 700-square-foot Manhattan loft. Downtown warehouse spaces like this are the urban equivalent of the country barn: architectural shells where arrangements are based on function. No matter how airy the loft feels, however, space is at a premium. To keep the floor plan flexible, Liz uses a trick of stage design. She hangs dramatic ceiling-to-floor curtains that, when drawn, form cozy conversation nooks, a private bedroom, guest bed, and intimate dining area. The result carves out a sense of mystery as well as expanse because, as Liz explains, "closed curtains give the idea that there's space yet to come."

In Liz's fantasy world, that space beyond would reveal a Parisian cityscape or her favorite church, St. Sulpice, in the Latin Quarter district where she lived while studying in France. Dove gray, the color of aging monuments, serves as the cornerstone of her paint palette, brightened by white walls, floors, and upholstery and alternately emboldened or softened with shades of blue. Toile de Jouy prints, depicting scenes of French life, skirt the bed and curtain the sleeping area; the treatment recalls a grand tradition of matching bed and wall hangings that goes back to the Sun King himself. Touches of gold, suggesting royal elegance, appear on a Louis XVI-style armchair and giltwood mirror.

OPPOSITE: **All the loft is a stage, with dramatic floor-to-ceiling curtains revealing or concealing distinct living spaces. Seating is arranged for cozy conversation, but chairs are casually mismatched and steeped in a pure country palette of easy whites and naturals. The crystal pendant chandelier, vintage brass candelabra, baroque garden sculpture, and strings of Christmas lights mesh downtown kitsch with French formality.** RIGHT: **An octagonal bamboo table adds warm color and natural texture.**
FAR RIGHT: **Leopard prints, a hallmark of the French Empire period, add a touch of luxury to the pared-down decor.**

BELOW LEFT: A bold, striped fabric updates an old fauteuil, or open-arm chair. A classical garden urn filled with Mexican ornaments adds cross-cultural flair to a rococo look. BELOW RIGHT: An alcove seating area doubles as the guest room. "Close the curtains, and it feels like you're traveling on a train," says Liz. A gilt mirror and chandelier hung high to reflect natural light add to the drama. OPPOSITE: A long country farm table updated with a coat of dove gray paint teams up with mismatched chairs from a Montreal thrift shop. Painting the floors a distressed white is a Swedish-style solution for enhancing the feeling of light in the space.

It's the simplicity of the loft that draws the eye to these flourishes. The long room is a blank canvas, against which new and old classics stand out with off-the-shoulder elegance. A crystal-pendant chandelier hangs along with the bare bulbs of a "suspendue" lamp and holiday lights. White duck—the same fabric used for artist's canvas—slipcovers French Country chairs, subtly hinting at their graceful lines. "Covering these old shapes makes them seem modern," notes Liz, who aims for the look of a sculptor's atelier, where backgrounds are kept raw and objects appear in high relief. A tarnished candelabra, crystal decanter, or exposed radiator are as sculpturally poignant in this setting as a statue of the goddess Diana Liz found in Brooklyn. Truly eclectic and highly romantic, the loft is a dreamy escape that traverses centuries and continents. "When you live in a hectic city," she says, "you need to come home to a place that's peaceful."

Liz freely pairs her grandmother's delicate rose and gilt-edged Bavarian china with heavier pieces of ironstone she bought at local shops and flea markets. Ironstone, a white earthenware, was developed in England in the early 1800s as an economical alternative to fine china. For the English market, ironstone was decorated with colorful designs, but for export to America and Europe, it was left plain. OPPOSITE: A cloudlike combination of dove gray, white, sterling silver, and clear crystal creates an ethereal effect at the table.

In this light and airy setting, the warm wood of
an **American Empire** sideboard provides a visual
anchor for the space. Propping an unframed
antique painting on the sideboard is a casual
alternative to hanging art on the wall. The silver
dome is an old hotel piece, bought at a flea
market in London, while the tall altar
candlestick is from an antiques shop in
Montreal. Painting the wall one-third gray adds
architectural interest; drawing the curtain
behind the sideboard suggests the feeling of a
corner niche.

## accenting with antiques

"I don't own a single thing that's new," says Liz Pierce, who seeks out bargains in thrift shops and antiques markets around the world. Here are a few of her favorites.

• Old books, specifically French paperbacks. Liz collects only those with creamy white covers accented with red and black typography for the visual impact they have as a group.

• Textiles. Remnants are great bargains, as are slightly damaged piece goods. Her favorite for adding a French accent: toile de Jouy prints, especially in blue and white.

• Glassware, silver, and china. She likes to mix her grandmother's hand-me-downs with street finds to set a table or create a tableau that looks as though it has been in the household for generations.

OPPOSITE: **Liz left the lady's French armchair as she found it, with upholstery torn and finish worn, to add a sense of history and integrity to the loft's dreamy decor. Leopard prints became popular during the Napoleonic era. Liz uses them as accents throughout the loft in a nod to history and for a touch of fashion and surprise.** BELOW: **A vintage brass candelabra, tarnished and with arms slightly bent, delights the eye with its graceful swirling curves.**

OPPOSITE: Red-and-white striped curtains lined with the same gray toile de Jouy used for the bed skirt define the sleeping area. An untucked white quilt breaks up the bedding's mix of pattern, which ranges from overscale checks to a leopard print. ABOVE: Built-in shelves hold an array of books and objets d'art. A utility lamp from a hardware store clamps to one edge of the built-in; it can be turned toward the bed for reading or into the corner for a wash of light. The antique burlwood chest adds monumentality with its stepped top and pillared sides. Mirrors on the shelves and wall reflect light and enhance the sense of space.

# ship shape

After years of renting cottages on New England's Martha's Vineyard, Judy and Jeff Naftulin began looking for a second home of their own. Unable to find the beachfront house of their dreams, they decided to build from scratch. Judy found a plot of land on the coast of Chappaquiddick with a view of busy Edgartown harbor in the distance. A two-ferry ride from the Massachusetts coast, Chappaquiddick is a secluded spot. The couple originally considered a very rustic retreat, but as Judy watched the harbor's yachts sail past, she found new inspiration. "I wanted something like a boat," she explains, "sleek and well-fitted, combining summery whites with dark polished woods."

Boating proved an apt analogy for the house, which was built on stilts, seemingly floating on a grassy bluff of unexpected dips and turns. Working with architects Mark Hutker and Peter Breese, Judy took the helm in the design, first deciding on highly lacquered, dark walnut floors and white walls, then on steel cables for the railings on the deck outside and along the inside stairwell. Steel cable also runs across the living room's soaring, 18-foot ceilings as a contemporary alternative to structural beams. Once the shell of the house was constructed, all else fell into place. Judy chose a palette of natural whites, beiges, and ever-deepening browns to blend the floors and walls, and took the scheme to its conclusion with black—on

OPPOSITE: **The black oak, barley-twist gateleg table is English; the cane-back wing chair was crafted in the 19th century on a Scottish isle. An overhead shelf sports a playful display of a salesman's sample hats piled like sculpture. The original hatbox turned on its side serves as a makeshift bookshelf.** RIGHT: **The house sits on stilts on a bluff above the shore. Cable railings give the illusion of standing on a ship's deck.** FAR RIGHT: **Natural tones and textures give warmth to the light-filled house. The 19th-century campaign chest in the foreground holds dining room linens.**

vintage-metal tole shades, a baby grand piano, and on new appliances and 1940s-style barstools in the kitchen. The black accents enrich the light-feeling space, while natural materials add a sense of comfort. Tactile surfaces range in texture rather than color, from smooth leather and brass to coarse burlap, worn woods, and rough sisal.

Antiques show a similar breadth of range. Judy freely mixes American country collectibles, such as a Shaker bed mat or an old wooden chocolate mold, with European pieces such as the English gateleg table and Scottish cane-back chair. Even more modern pieces, including 1930s leather club chairs, join the blend. Though the objects that grace her home come from many ports of call, Judy still runs a tight ship. Clutter is nonexistent. Like the yacht she used as inspiration, there's a place for everything and everything in its place.

**OPPOSITE: A Maine guide canoe rests overhead on structural steel cables (contemporary "beams") to break up the vertical expanse of soaring, 18-foot ceilings. A row of raffia fish baskets on the wall holds desk papers; an Ohio Shaker bed mat hangs over the mantel, which rests on two 19th-century pillars salvaged from a Southern mansion. BELOW: An appliqué spread and basic blue-and-tan mattress ticking dress the new platform bed. A folding outdoor table painted shiny black serves as a bedside table.**

TAKE OUT EAT IN

The kitchen mixes vintage modern and vintage country, pairing 1940s-style barstools and an over-the-window neon sign with a 19th-century whitewashed walnut table from a charcuterie in France. The table has a worn, unpolished marble top, while kitchen counters are new tumbled marble, rimmed in warm-toned walnut. Black appliances stand out in strong contrast; baskets, window shades, and an old chocolate mold over the stove add natural color and texture. All storage, including that for dishes and glassware, is below the counter. Judy avoided cabinetry above in favor of an unobstructed view of the landscape outside.

OPPOSITE: **An extra step in the master bath allows for a deeper tub. Long soaks are made all the more luxurious by the addition of a silver candelabra, elegantly bottled bath oils, and the exaggerated enlargement of Leonardo da Vinci's** *Mona Lisa*, **painted on wood by a contemporary Canadian artist. The nearby chair, used here with a terry cloth pillow, has a companion in the guest bath.** ABOVE: **Antique, brown-transferware plates fill a wall in the guest bath, where countertops are laid in the same dark walnut as the floors. The French boudoir chair is slipcovered in heavy white cotton denim, impervious to wet bathers. Placing furniture in the bathroom takes the space beyond the utilitarian and makes it feel lived in.**

Judy decorated the bedrooms of daughters, Kiira, age 16, and Jenny, age 21, as colorful complements of one another. The rooms have a connecting door and share an outdoor deck. Beds have trundles (useful for overnight guests) and new quilts. Bamboo shades and wicker tables continue the natural scheme of the house, while plastic lamps with tangerine and lilac shades that match the colors of the butterfly chairs add modern flair.

## study in contrasts

With a coffee-and-cream color scheme tying everything together, Judy plays up contrasting textures and styles for dynamic interest.

• Stripped, weathered wood columns add aged patina to a freshly painted white fireplace.

• The leather on vintage club chairs offers smooth, touchable texture in contrast to the nubby upholstery fabric used on an overscaled ottoman.

• A sleek photographer's umbrella lamp serves as lighting sculpture in a white bedroom, where loose pillows in a range of weaves add bold accents.

• A combination of fabrics in soft and coarse fibers updates the appearance of antique dark-oak chairs.

# rules of order

Mary Emmerling first fell in love with Santa Fe in the early 1980s, when she traveled there to research her first book on American country decorating. Having lived on the East Coast, she was drawn to the mountains, the soil, the adobe, and the other-worldly sun that casts an unmatched glow over it all. "My grandparents were from Wyoming," she says, "so the West is in my blood." When a two-room adobe house came up for sale, Mary made a mental note of it. Years later, she contacted a real estate agent. "If that little house is ever for sale," she said, "let me know." The answer? "It's on the market right now." The space measures just 850 square feet, with a living area, kitchen, bath, and bedroom. But thanks to Mary's conviction about keeping everything organized and using items that serve double duty, the small space is immensely livable. It also conveys the lively Southwestern lifestyle she loves. "It's always an adventure here," Mary says. "We can do something different every day: hiking, fishing up in the mountains, going to a dance or fiesta. It's all about having fun and celebrating."

That lightness of spirit is reflected in Mary's home, inside and out. At 7,000 feet, Santa Fe sits in the high desert, a surprisingly ideal climate for roses and hollyhocks. Mary has started a lavender garden on the side, near a picket fence that's as pristine as the adobe is sun-baked. That fence, she says, stands as a symbol of the marriage of country and continued on page 164

OPPOSITE: **The natural textures and colors of country blend easily in the living room, where Mary Emmerling combined the collections of her past with folk art native to the Southwest. The leopard prints mix well with Navajo geometric patterns. Religious artifacts reflect the history of the region. "The Southwest," Mary says, "is about the soul."** RIGHT: **At the back of the house, Mexican doors open up the adobe wall that encloses an outdoor entertaining area.** FAR RIGHT: **A lavender garden greets visitors at the side of the adobe house.**

The simple backdrop of adobe offers visual space for an extensive collection of artifacts. New candelabras over the fireplace provide plenty of opportunities for soft candlelight; the painting is a Santa Fe landscape by a local artist. Underfoot, sisal rugs soften the brick floor. The French mirror from an East Coast department store makes the room look bigger than it is and reflects the patio outside.

**BELOW LEFT:** Wicker chairs and baskets (including an oversize one that serves as a coffee table) bring a casual feeling to the living room. **BELOW RIGHT:** An elaborately carved architectural fragment finds new life as sculpture. **OPPOSITE:** The kitchen makes up for its small size with its ample cupboard space. Mary keeps everyday items at hand, displaying fruit on ironstone platters and in baskets and placing utensils and bottles of wine in other baskets nearby. The painting over the doorway, a typical example of Southwestern folk art, "hides something ugly," Mary says.

Southwestern style. Inside the house, she has blended the two with her signature style, bringing baskets and wooden furnishings from the East and accessorizing them with everything from Navajo blankets to turquoise jewelry. "It all mixes so easily," she says.

That effortless blend is a hallmark of the new country style, which combines furnishings and accessories from different cultures, regions, and periods of history. "It's all about being influenced by where you are," Mary says. "Surround yourself with things that have meaning for you, no matter where they come from." In this Santa Fe house, ironstone platters and New England baskets share space with Peruvian silver and Southwestern landscape paintings. "Even the cowboy clothes are easy to mix in," Mary says. "They fit with the collecting I've done my whole life."

In keeping with her philosophy of organizing collections by type to give them greater impact, Mary piles Stetson and straw hats in a basket. They, like everything else, serve double duty, being both decorative and handy when Mary and her husband, Reg Jackson, leave for a flea market or hike. "At this altitude," she says, "you have to wear a hat." Hanging necklaces from pegs on the bathroom wall not only organizes her jewelry and keeps it in easy reach, but also makes a colorful display. A medallion known as a milagro (Spanish for "miracle") hangs above the jewelry.

ABOVE LEFT AND RIGHT: **Organization is the key to living in a small space, and one way to achieve it is to arrange functional items—such as jewelry, clothing, and cosmetics—in ways that are both orderly and visually pleasing. A handwrought iron peg holds a variety of necklaces in the bathroom, while Indian baskets filled with silver and turquoise jewelry bring soft color and richness to the bedroom.**

ABOVE: **A Mexican serape brightens the small bedroom, which is accented with Southwestern details. A white quilt and crisp white sheets dress the ornate Italian bed, which features a gilded wood and velvet headboard. Animal-print and vintage floral print pillows accent the bed and an old wicker chair. The blue saint figure in the window came from New Mexico; a collection of brass, tin, and silver milagros hangs under the framed artwork. Mexican silver frames fill the bedside table. "A house is not a home without candles, flowers, and pictures of your family," Mary says.**

## dressing up country

Mary Emmerling feels there's a yin and yang to new country style, meaning that rustic and opulent can stand side by side. Here are a few ways to achieve that mix.

• Look for silver vases and mirror frames from Mexico—they are more detailed than those from New England, and they bring a subtle sheen to the room.

• Check antiques shops for candle stands, such as floor candles from a church altar. They add drama and height as well as the warmth of candlelight.

• Be creative in repurposing items. A 1950s cosmetics case made of Mexican etched leather is the right size for weekend videos.

• Use framed, black-and-white photographs to provide sophisticated contrast to the warm hues of leather and leopard skin.

# melting pot

Imagine a living room 35 feet long in a house with 5,500 square feet of space to fill, and two young boys who have been known to play basketball indoors. Faced with those challenges in her Tucson residence, Mary Mulcahy has used fabric, secondhand furnishings, and creative inspiration from all over the world to make the house a comfortable home. Fabrics from France, tile from Mexico, and rugs from Morocco prove that the world of decorating is a harmonious place after all. And by using many "previously owned" items, Mary incorporates the make-do spirit of American country, using her imagination and creativity to transform the constantly changing canvas of her home.

The house, a 1929 Spanish Colonial, caught her eye for the same reason she's often drawn to thrift store furniture: It had bold lines and unlimited potential. "It's a big, old house with classic interiors—wood floors, thick plaster walls, and lots of details, such as cove moldings, chair rails, and paneled wood doors that you don't generally find here," she says. A seasoned traveler and former New York resident, Mary has frequented big-city boutiques and Paris flea markets. Now she explores the local Goodwill and Salvation Army stores. "I wouldn't dignify any of the places I go with the term 'antiques store,' " she says. "I can tell if a piece has really good bones. It's fun to find something that looks hopeless, but that you know can be saved with some TLC."

OPPOSITE: White cotton slipcovers give new life to a reproduction French sofa, a $30 thrift-store bargain. Plump feather pillows soften the sofa's long lines; the blue-and-white pillow fabric is from Paris. Shutters frame the windows for a country touch. RIGHT: Inspired by columnlike fountains she had seen in France, Mary designed the one that stands in front of the guesthouse and had it made by stonemasons in Mexico. FAR RIGHT: Architectural details, such as the tile roof, give the house a Mediterranean attitude. In keeping with that feeling, an old metal bed plumped with pillows serves as an outdoor chaise for afternoon naps; bright-colored cloths accent tables and chairs.

To adapt her house to her family's needs, Mary assessed the space and introduced a few innovations. The 35-foot living room, for instance, is divided into three areas: a conversational grouping, office space, and a guest bedroom. To add height to the long room with a theatrical flair, she suspended yards of fabric from a hand-carved architectural element salvaged from a Mexican church. That global quality in new country decorating honors the universal folk art traditions of different cultures. At the same time, this expert in international relations also fashions slipcovers for one practical and thoroughly domestic reason: "I can have my French fabrics," she says, "and I don't have to worry about them."

OPPOSITE: The blue-and-white color scheme, used throughout the large room, ties together the living area, guest space, and office. A traditional palette for American country, blue and white take on an international flavor with French-inspired fabrics and animal prints. An oversize ottoman doubles as a coffee table. BELOW: A daybed with draperies hung from an antique cornice dramatically turns one end of the 35-foot room into a space for guests. Classic country fabrics, such as ticking, gingham, and stripes, look fresh when combined with lots of white.

Vivid yellow walls and a dark wood floor create an air of intimacy and European style in the dining room. Layers of cloths cover the dining table to suggest elegance and opulence. (The same trick works with blankets on the bed and pillows on the sofa.) Fabrics bought in Paris cover the seats of the Swedish-style chairs. Mary's friend, artist Paula Hamilton, painted the walls freehand with an 18th-century chinoiserie pattern, mimicking that of the crystal chandelier, and Mary used the same source of inspiration to design the wooden candelabra on the side table.

OPPOSITE: An upstairs bedroom for Mary's sons demonstrates the mix of thrift-store finds and personal preferences. Mary freshened the beds with a coat of paint, found a new top for an old desk, and covered a yard-sale chair with vintage gingham. BELOW: For the master bedroom, Mary paid $20 for the headboard at a thrift store and had it covered to coordinate with the blue-striped taffeta quilt, another Paris find. Under the quilt she layers cotton sheets and coverlets for a look of richness. A new caned love seat stands on an animal-print rug, a sophisticated accent that keeps her country look fresh.

**BELOW: A tall-back sofa found in Montreal wears a cameo print.** OPPOSITE TOP AND BOTTOM RIGHT: **In the work area, a handpainted room divider defines space. Slipcovers for all upholstered pieces let Mary change the color temperature in the room. During the hot Arizona summers, she uses a soothing blue-and-white palette; in the winter, she switches to hot reds and pinks.** OPPOSITE BOTTOM LEFT: **In the bath, pressed-concrete tiles, handcrafted in Mexico, cover the floor. Black-and-white French toile upholsters the secondhand chair. An old Mexican tin lamp and a chandelier supply light.**

To combine regional items and fabrics from all over the world, follow these guidelines.

• Color can be the great unifier. Determine a color scheme that's traditionally used in other parts of the world. Blue and white, for instance, is a standard in American country decorating, but it's also popular in French country style.

• Don't be afraid to mix. "I like to see an old table and a modern lamp, animal prints with ginghams," Mary says. "Too much of one thing looks too cute to me."

• Look for basic pieces that can work in a variety of settings, such as open-arm chairs or mirrors framed in everything from weathered wood to ornate molding.

• Introduce distinctive architectural salvage pieces as decorative elements.

# personal design strategies

Allow your passions, hobbies, cultural interests, or personal history to be your guides as you weave varied elements into a harmonious whole. Let your personality define your country style by following these simple guidelines.

**Personal country** design schemes are a bit like plot lines, developing character through carefully choreographed vignettes. Start with a piece you love or that has personal meaning and build from there.

**Add visual depth by** displaying favorite objects on all available surfaces, from cabinets, tabletops, and mantels to walls, floors, ceilings, and stair landings. Create tableaus with candles and vases grouped in front of paintings, or drape your grandmother's shawl over the back of a slipcovered chair. Layer similar objects, such as matching plates in a cupboard, to lend stability or provide contrasting textures, colors, or forms to build rhythm.

**Before nailing another** picture to the wall, question traditional choices and think about where else it could go—perhaps hanging in front of a

### multiplicity

**LEFT:** Instead of placing two or three plates on a shelf, fill each shelf with a different set of dishes. Order arrangements by color and size to create the effect of symmetry from mismatched objects; two duck decoys, for example, balance two framed prints. **ABOVE:** Anything of beauty is worthy of display, including wardrobe accessories, such as this silver and turquoise jewelry.

## orderly display

RIGHT: See-through wire racks allow artful displays to be seen from every corner of the room. Shelves hold a mix of collectibles and household items, the less sculptural of which are stored in attractive baskets. Books are stacked in tabletop groupings, anchored by taller objects, such as the brass candlesticks and model ship.

## balancing act

LEFT: Six framed prints neatly stacked in gridlike fashion help balance bulkier furniture pieces, such as the cupboard and blue-painted barrel. Not all frame moldings are alike; alternating rows of wood and gold frames add visual interest to the orderly arrangement.

## self-expression

LEFT: Instead of hiding cowboy boots in the closet, line them up in the hall.
ABOVE: Add off-the-shoulder elegance to a small bathroom with a dressy chandelier and primitive cupboard.
RIGHT: Southwestern bultos (carved saints) were fashioned to be ritually adorned with an ever-changing array of costumes and jewelry.

bookcase or leaning against the backsplash of your kitchen counter. Three-dimensional objects can likewise decorate walls, adding architectural interest above a doorway or window. Avoid predictabilty by mixing what's new and old, warm and cool, coarse and fine, or priceless and bargain-basement. Design that caters to you should also make daily tasks easier. Keep essentials within reach in containers worthy of display themselves. Leave room on the coffee table for tired feet, and always have the courage to edit your belongings.

## the layered look

RIGHT: **Create comfort by layering pillows over throws over slipcovered chairs to turn a formal wingback into an easy chair.** BELOW: **A primitive cupboard's doorknobs offer a handy place to hang Southwestern silver chains and pendants. The old farm cupboard could be from anywhere, but adorned with jewelry and paired with the Native American throw rug and a row of Western boots, the piece exudes local pride. Peeling paint, aged woods, worn leather, woven textiles, and silver range in texture from smooth to coarse and dull to shiny.**

## get organized

BELOW: **The more elements and objects you have in a home, the more important it is to keep them orderly and organized. Storage inside an armoire shows how sorted groupings create a design pattern of their own. Arrange belts and other items that cannot be neatly stacked in low baskets and put them on an eye-level shelf for visibility. Doorknobs serve as makeshift pegs for hanging beaded and fringed purses.**

## adaptive use

**ABOVE:** Any surface can work as a desktop, provided there's storage space to compensate for drawers; here the baskets and bowls used to hold office supplies work as an attractive display in themselves.
**BELOW:** A folding screen behind the bed shows off a changing display of small photos or souvenirs.

## creative repurposing

**ABOVE:** The floor is a surface as serviceable as a tabletop, especially when you're on the couch. Use dough bowls or even an old punch bowl under tables to hold photos or magazines. **LEFT:** Gather paintbrushes or pencils in a mustard crock or jelly jar. **BELOW:** Straw hats become whimsical sculpture when piled to look as if their pyramidal display had just fallen, giving multiple views of the same object.

# sources

## BIG STYLE COUNTRY

Page 8: Bed—American Country Collection, 620 Cerrillos Rd., Santa Fe, NM 87501; 505/984-0955. Table, antique—Foreign Traders, 202 Galisteo St., Santa Fe, NM 87501; 505/983-6441; www.foreigntraders.com. Navajo rugs—Streets of Taos, 505/983-8268.

Page 10: Architect—Laban Wingert Associates, Architects, P.O. Box 2045, Santa Fe, NM 87504; 505/983-7200. Ceiling paint #799—Benjamin Moore & Co. For nearest store, call 800/826-2623; www.benjaminmoore.com. Navajo rug—Streets of Taos, 505/983-8268. Black-and-white photographs—Douglas Kent Hall, 505/343-0989; www.douglaskenthall.com. Art lighting, Joshua—Tech Lighting Galleries, 300 W. Superior, Chicago, IL 60610; 312/642-1586.

Page 14: Tub, Epoque by American Standard—Porcher, 800/359-3261. Faucet, Madison—Dornbracht USA, Inc., 800/774-1181.

Page 15: Vanity designed by Laban Wingert—Custom Hardware, 947 W. Alameda, Santa Fe, NM 87501; 505/984-0879. Faucet #RFC1010—Soho Corporation, 800/969-7647.

Pages 16-17: Table, custom—Foreign Traders, 202 Galisteo, Santa Fe, NM 87501; 505/983-6441; www.foreigntraders.com. Chairs—Artesanos Imports Co., 505/983-1743; www.artesanos.com. Cabinets designed by Laban Wingert—Robert S. Pepper, Cabinetmakers Inc., P.O. Box 5604, Santa Fe, NM 97502; 505/471-0500.

Page 19: (Top right) Cowboy-fabric footstool—Cry Baby Ranch, 888/279-2229; www.crybabyranch.com.

## RUGGED INDIVIDUALISM

Pages 20-29: Architect—Brian E. Boyle, AIA, 75 Spring St., 6th Floor, New York, NY 10012; 212/334-7402. Interior design—Zina Glazebrook, Z.G. Design, 10 Wireless Rd., East Hampton, NY 11937; 631/329-7486; fax 631/329-2087; www.zgdesign.com. Painted furniture—Monique Shay Antiques, 920 Main St. S., Woodbury, CT 06798; 203/263-3186. Lighting—Architrove, 74 Montauk Hwy., East Hampton, NY 11937; 631/329-2229. Vases, containers—Hunters and Collectors, Montauk Highway, Box 1932, Bridgehampton, NY 11932; 631/537-4233.

Page 20: Linens—Bagley Home, 155 Main St., Sag Harbor, NY 11963; 631/725-3553.

Page 22: (Left) Wall paint #2026-50 Fresh Cut Grass—Benjamin Moore & Co. For nearest store, call 800/826-2623; www.benjaminmoore.com.

Page 24: Portrait—For more information on the artist, Howard Finster, visit www.finster.com.

## PURE & SIMPLE

Pages 30-39: Antiques—McCormick Art & Antiques, 214 W. St. Louis St., Lebanon, IL 62254; 618-537-8392.

## NEW BLUE DESIGN STRATEGIES

Page 40: (Left) Ceramics (from left): #BNSCT Radial Cream/Sugar, tank (Sugar at far right); #N3B Bud, black; #MOKOGP Teardrop, petrol; #N7B Large Bowl, black; #R29 Gulp, tobacco—Jonathan Adler, 212/941-8950; www.jonathanadler.com. (Right) Sideboard #476, from Monogram collection—The Lane Co., Inc. For nearest store, call 800/750-5263; www.lanefurniture.com. Paint #TH04B Cameo—Ralph Lauren Paints, 800/379-7656.

Page 41: (Top left) Love seat #484-3 Thatcher—Norwalk Furniture Corp. Throw, Alpaca wool, rye—Archipelago, 212/334-9460. Cushion, dune white—The Terence Conran Shop, 212/755-9079; www.conran.com. (Top right) Chairs #657973 Bellini; bowl #597179—The Terence Conran Shop (see above). Light fixture, Fisherman's Lamp—Pottery Barn, 800/922-5507; www.potterybarn.com. Paint #SF17B Pueblo—Ralph Lauren Paints (see under Page 40). (Center) Bed #770 Pencil post, burnished-oil finish, from Natural Transitions collection—Harden Furniture Co. For nearest store, call 315/245-1000; www.harden.com. White quilt, Jaya, hand-stitched—Pine Cone Hill, 413/496-9700; www.pineconehill.com. Blanket, Basketweave, allium—Calvin Klein Home. For nearest store, call 800/294-7978. Throw, Alpaca, mist—Archipelago (see above). Pillows on window seat (front to back): Hydrangea stitched, larkspur—Archipelago (see above); Embroidered Dots, violet—Calvin Klein Home (see above); Euro alpaca, mist; suede, lilac—Archipelago (see above). (Bottom left) Floor lamp, Best Light, ecru shade and base—The Terence Conran Shop (see above).

Page 42: (Top) Blue mugs (in cabinet) #597062—The Terence Conran Shop (see under Page 41). Plates two-tone, creme—Eigen Arts. Available at Tesori, 888/903-9400. (Bottom) Chandelier #6905 The Cambridge, wrought-iron, antique black—Areo, 888/814-7988; www.areohome.com. Glasses, St. Augustine, hand-blown 18th-century reproduction—Period Designs, 757/886-9482; www.perioddesigns.com. Glass bowl #436 Extra Large Windsor Bowl—Simon Pearce, 888/774-5277; www.simonpearceglass.com. Basket (under table) #K30/N30 Adirondack basket, leather handles,

natural—Basketville, 800/258-4553; www.basketville.com. Wicker dining chair #3201 Casa Grande, sage—Lloyd/Flanders, 888/227-8252; www.lloydflanders.com. Paint #SA17A Cairo—Ralph Lauren Paints (see under Page 40).

Page 43: (Top right) Sofa #264-003T-2 Avalon Bench, fabric #29044 Erin, mist—Mitchell Gold, 800/789-5401; www.mitchellgold.com. Yellow pillows, Alpaca, rye; throw (on sofa) Alpaca, sage—Archipelago (see under page 41). Satin pillow, Ginko silk satin, hand-stitched—Ann Gish Inc., 805/498-4447. Hexagonal table #6140-60, tobacco, from Winterthur Country Estate collection—Hickory Chair Co., 800/349-4579; www.hickorychair.com. Earthenware bowl, Salad Bowl, mushroom—Potluck Studios. For nearest dealer, call 845/626-2300; www.potluckstudios.com. (Center) Wing chair #7261-83h, cushion #7355-63H saddle leather, brown, from Sweater Weave collection—Palecek. For nearest store, call 800/274-7730; www.palecek.com. (Bottom left) Pitcher #597070—The Terence Conran Shop (see under Page 41). (Bottom right) Love seat #729-02 Harlington, Vineyard Check fabric, chambray—Ralph Lauren Home, 800/578-7656.

Page 44: Coverlets Kreta, green—The Garnet Hill Catalog, 800/622-6216; www.garnethill.com.

## BY THE SEA

Page 46: Designer—Judy Naftulin, 215/297-0702. Bamboo shades—Smith+Noble Window Treatments. For catalog, call 800/765-7776; www.smithandnoble.com.

Page 49: Chair upholstery fabric White Denim—Shabby Chic, 800/876-3226.

## SOUVENIRS & KEEPSAKES

Page 54: Chairs by Old Hickory—Available from Camps and Cottages, 1231 North Coast Highway, Laguna Beach, CA 92651; 949/376-8474.

Page 56: Coffee table—Steve Reed Painted American Country Furniture, 510/233-4624. Also available from Camps and Cottages (see under Page 54).

Page 61: Pillow fabric—Country House Fabrics, 805/482-2006; www.countryhousefabrics.com. Quilt by J. Clayton International—Available from Camps and Cottages (see under Page 54). Sign—Steve Reed Painted American Country Furniture (see under Page 56).

Page 62: Bed, Shutter Bed—Maine Cottage Furniture, 207/846-1430; www.mainecottage.com.

Page 63: Cupboard—Steve Reed Painted American Country Furniture (see under Page 56).

## RELAXED & ROMANTIC

Pages 64-75: Interior design—Sue Balmforth, 1335 Abbot Kinney Blvd., Venice, CA 90291; 310/450-3620. Antiques, architectural artifacts, furnishings, and floral design—Bountiful, 1335 Abbot Kinney Blvd., Venice, CA 90291; 310/450-3620; www.bountiful-online.com. Hardwood floors—Marina Flooring, 3121 Washington Blvd., Marina Del Rey, CA 90292; 310/821-3344. Window coverings—Karin Nukk, 16449 Dearborn St., North Hills, CA 91343; 818/892-7821. Slipcovers and upholstery—Monte Allen, 2326 Centinela Ave., West Los Angeles, CA 90064; 310/207-7676.

Page 68: Light fixtures, Fisherman's Lamp, aluminum—Pottery Barn, 800/922-5507; www.potterybarn.com.

Page 71: Pillows—Kevin Simon Clothing, 1358 Abbot Kinney Blvd., Venice, CA 90291; 310/392-4630; www.kevinsimonclothing.com. Bed lamps designed by Penni Oliver—Bountiful (see under Pages 64-75). Lampshades—Carl's Custom Lamps and Shades, 8334 Beverly Blvd., Los Angeles, CA 90048; 323/651-5825.

## OCEAN COLORS

Pages 76-87: Fabrics throughout—Room Service by Ann Fox, 4354 Lovers Lane, Dallas, TX 75225; 214/369-7666. Vintage pillows throughout—Fran Bennett Design, 1009 Park Ave., Spring Lake Heights, NJ 07762; 732/449-8431.

Pages 80-81: Dining chairs, sconces, compote—Room Service by Ann Fox (see under Pages 76-87). Vintage buffet, iron chairs—Beverley Brown Antiques, 511 Bay Ave., Point Pleasant Beach, NJ 08742; 732/899-9303.

Page 83: Iron bed, vintage bedspreads—Room Service by Ann Fox (see under Pages 76-87).

Page 84: (Left) Antique chest and mirror—Antiques on Bay, 513 Bay Ave., Point Pleasant Beach, NJ 08742; 732/295-4113.

Page 85: Toile fabric #662122 Country Life Vintage, lake—Waverly, 800/423-5881; www.waverly.com. Also available through Room Service by Ann Fox (see under Pages 76-87).

Page 87: Vintage pillowcases, tablecloths—Room Service by Ann Fox (see under Pages 76-87).

## COTTAGE DESIGN STRATEGIES

Page 88: Vintage fabrics—The Marston House Antiques, Main Street at Middle, Box 517, Wiscasset, ME 04578; 207/882-6010.

Page 89: (Right) Wicker dining chairs #8001 and #8007 (with full skirt), from Heirloom collection—Lloyd/Flanders, 888/227-8252; www.lloydflanders.com. Carpet squares, maize—Pier 1 Imports, Inc. For nearest store, call 800/245-4595; www.pier1.com. Antiques—The Marston House Antiques (see under Page 88) and Treillage Ltd., 418 E. 75th St., New York, NY 10021; 212/535-2288. Wicker sofa #5000-33, #84 hunter green finish; chaise lounge #5000-77, #84 hunter green finish; both from Aquarius collection—Lexington Home Brands, 800/539-4636; www.lexington.com.

Page 91: (Top left) Chandelier, Bountiful (see under Pages 64–75). Wicker sofa, Lexington Home Brands (see under Page 89). (Bottom left) Fabric, Room Service by Ann Fox (see under Pages 76–87). Vintage pillow, Fran Bennett Design (see under Pages 76–87).

## LOG CABIN REVIVAL

Pages 94–107: Homespun fabrics throughout—The Red Rooster, 1001 W. Main St., Greenfield, IN 46140; 317/462-0655. Paint: Cupboards #1701 New England Red; floors #1710 Golden Mustard; doors and windows #1703 Pearwood, all acrylic latex, soft sheen, interior and exterior—Old Village Paints Ltd., 800/498-7687; www.old-village.com. Chandelier—Katie's Light House, 5320 Beeler Rd., Cridersville, OH 45806; 419/222-4520.

Page 95: (Left) Basket by Trevle Wood, 1623 Lewis Circle, Murfreesboro, TN 37129; 615/895-0391.

Page 98: Stencil #FS14F2-2 Bump Tavern Design—MB Historic Décor, 888/649-1790; www.communityinfo.com/stencils.

Page 99: Thumb latch, hinges—Jerry Bolinger, Homestead Shops & Gardens, 1866 E. 1400 N, North Manchester, IN 46962; 219/982-2829.

Page 101: Sconce—Katie's Light House (see under Pages 94–107).

Page 102: Chandelier—Katie's Light House (see under Pages 94–107).

Page 103: Lanterns—Katie's Light House (see under Pages 94–107).

## MODERN SALTBOX

Page 108: Windsor chairs, reproduction—Farmhouse Antiques, 2816 Ave. D, Nederland, TX 77627; 409/727-4017. Settle, antique—MacKay & Field, 860/455-1055.

Page 109: House plans #25.1 The Sheepscot House, #68 The Woodbury House—McKie Roth Design, 800/232-7684; www.mckieroth.com. Shingles, Independence Shangles in Weathered Wood—CertainTeed, 800/782-8777; www.certainteed.com.

Page 110: Windsor chairs, reproduction—Farmhouse Antiques (see under Page 108).

Page 112: Cupboard, antique—MacKay & Field (see under Page 108).

Page 113: Paint: Walls, Roxbury Tavern Red; floor, Ditty Box Mustard—Sharon Platt American Antiques and Historic Paint Colours, 1347 Rustic View, Manchester, MO 63011; 636/227-5304.

Page 114: Paint: Cabinets, Higham House Brown; floor, Stonington Gray—Sharon Platt American Antiques and Historic Paint Colours (see under Page 113). Lighting fixtures (right front) #40202 Pembrook (right rear) #30071 Revere Tavern-Rising Sun pattern, distressed finish—Lt. Moses Willard. For nearest dealer, call 513/248-5500.

Page 115: Bed, reproduction—Farmhouse Antiques (see under Page 108). Blanket chest, antique—MacKay & Field (see under Page 108). Linen blanket (available trundle to king size), pillowcase, apron, curtains: period reproduction garments and bed linens—1803 Homespun, 14800 Brawley Rd., Amesville, OH 45711; 740/448-7360; www.1803homespun.com.

Pages 116–117: Wing chair, Woodstock—The Seraph, 800/737-2742; www.theseraph.com. Windsor chair, reproduction—Farmhouse Antiques (see under Page 108). Wall paint, East Chamber Green—Sharon Platt American Antiques and Historic Paint Colours (see under Page 113). Sign, reproduction—MacKay & Field (see under Page 108).

## HOME TO HERITAGE

Page 118: Table—Brian Stringer Antiques, 2031 W. Alabama, Houston, TX 77098; 713/526-7380. Light fixture—Adele Kerr Furnishings, 214/741-4850.

Page 120: (Left) Twig mirror—La Lune Collection, 414/263-5300. (Right) Milk tin lamp—The Sitting Room, 2402 Quenby, Houston, TX 77005; 713/523-1932; www.thesittingroom.net.

Page 122: Rug—Creative Flooring Resources, 713/522-1181. Ottoman, London—George C. Nash, 214/744-1544. Sofa, Knightsbridge, ticking stripe; leather club chairs, topiaries—The Sitting Room (see under Page 120). Pine dresser—Brian Stringer Antiques (see under Page 118). Boot lamp—Carol Gibbins Antiques, 1817 Woodhead St., Houston, TX 77019; 713/524-9011. Table, ladder-back chairs—Carl Moore Antiques, 1610 Bissonnet, Houston, TX 77005; 713/524-2502.

Page 123: Butcher's table, antique—The Whimsey Shop, 2923 N. Henderson, Dallas, TX 75206; 214/824-6300. Basket, chest, antique—The Sitting Room (see under Page 120).

Page 125: Bench fabric #8285 Holcomb, beige—Pindler & Pindler. For nearest showroom, call 805/531-9090. Quilt, antique—The Sitting Room (see under Page 120).

Page 127: Island, custom—Carol Gibbins Antiques (see under Page 122). Dough bowl, barstools—Brian Stringer Antiques (see under Page 118). Carved deer—The Sitting Room (see under Page 120).

Kilim rug, antique—Carol Piper Rugs, 1809 W. Gray, Houston, TX 77019; 713/524-2442. Dome lights, custom—Alcon Light Craft Co., 713/526-0680.

Pages 128–129: Wicker furniture, quilt, cages, antique—The Sitting Room (see under Page 120).

## RUSTIC DESIGN STRATEGIES

Page 130: (Left) Sideboard #527-62 Legacy, cherry finish, Williamsburg collection—The Lane Co., Inc. For nearest store, call 800/750-5263; www.lanefurniture.com. (Right) Bench #486-29, #485 northwest cherry finish, Eddie Bauer collection—The Lane Co., Inc. (see above). Coatrack #9188 Double Costumer, cherry finish—Stickley Furniture, 315/682-5500; www.stickley.com.

Page 131: (Top left) Rattan sofa #7056-63H, walnut finish, #7398-17H bisque cushion; chair #7765-63H, walnut finish, #7391-17H bisque cushion; coffee table #7769-63H, walnut finish, all from President's Collection—Palecek. For nearest store, call 800/274-7730; www.palecek.com. Tea table #17.907.1 Malacca, pine solids with crackle lacquer finish—Milling Road, 800/592-2537; www.millingroad.com. Ottoman, Mercer, Hawaii-Bosc leather—Mitchell Gold, 800/789-5401; www.mitchellgold.com. Frames—Exposures Home, 877/805-5890; www.exposuresonline.com. Curtain rods #47-1074087, #47-1074095 adjustable curved iron—Pottery Barn, 800/922-5507; www.potterybarn.com. Wall lamp #269019—Gardeners Eden, 800/822-1214. (Top right) Server #833-867 Hinged-Top Cabinet—Lexington Home Brands, 800/539-4636; www.lexington.com. Entertainment center, Village Tapestry—Broyhill Furniture Industries, Inc., 800/327-6944; www.broyhillfurn.com. Wing chair, Host, mahogany finish—Hickory Chair Co., 800/349-4579; www.hickorychair.com. Throws (under server): left, Wool Lattice, tan and beige; center, Wool Woven Check, tan—Peacock Alley Luxury Linens, 800/810-0708; www.peacockalley.com; right, Sweater Knit, beige and charcoal—Good Home, 877/642-2487; www.goodhome.com. Curtain fabric, jute gauze—Rose Brand, 800/223-1624. Rug, ribbed jute—World Caravan, 818/623-0444. (Center) Sideboard #421-721, vintage finish, Town & Country collection—Century Furniture Industries, 800/852-5552; www.centuryfurniture.com. Floor lamp #9136L7 Square-based, cherry finish, linen shade—Stickley Furniture (see under Page 130). (Bottom left) Pottery—Potluck Studios. For nearest dealer, call 845/626-2300; www.potluckstudios.com. (Bottom right) Black-and-white wool plaid blanket #5051 Menzies Tartan Motor Robe—Pendleton Woolen Mills, 800/760-4844; www.pendleton-usa.com. Vintage blankets—Laura Fisher/Antique Quilts & Americana, 1050 Second Ave., Gallery 84, New York, NY 10022; 212/838-2596; Paula Rubenstein, Ltd., 212-966-8954.

Page 132: (Top) Black-and-white photograph—Michael Kahn, www.michaelkahn.com. Frame, Rutledge—Exposures Home (see under Page 131, Top Left). (Left) Side chairs #833-880 Chippendale, ivory crewel fabric seat—Lexington Home Brands (see under Page 131). Cotton throw (used as tablecloth), parchment—Calvin Klein Home. For nearest store, call 800/294-7978. (Right) Goblet #103 Bell; pitcher #370 Round—Simon Pearce, 888/774-5277; www.simonpearceglass.com. Flatware Gabriella, pewter—Match. Call 201/792-9444 for nearest retailer.

Page 133: (Top right) Cupboard #833-864 Kitchen pottery cupboard—Lexington Home Brands (see under Page 131, Top Right). Tall vase, molasses—Potluck Studios (see under Page 131, Bottom Left). (Bottom right) Sofa, Luc, brown leather—Restoration Hardware, 888/243-9720; www.restorationhardware.com.

Page 134: White upholstery fabric #647050 Heritage, white—Waverly; 800/423-5881; www.waverly.com.

## FRENCH CONNECTION

Page 139: Toile fabric, U-Letoile, color #15—Covington Fabrics, a division of Covington Industries Inc., 212/689-2200.

## SHIP SHAPE

Page 148: Seagrass coffee table #948-04 Payton Ottoman—Ralph Lauren Home. For nearest store, call 800/578-7656. Oriental rug, 19th century—Undercover/Underfoot, 10 Church St., Lambertville, NJ 08530; 609/397-0044.

Page 149: Painting by Louise Kamp, c. 1910—Arenskjold Antiques, 537 Warren St., Hudson, NY 12534; 518/828-2800.

Page 150: Canoe, reproduction—In the Woods, 55 Main St., Box 5095, Edgartown, MA 02539; 508/627-8989. Pilasters 19th century—Artefact, 215/794-8790; www.artefactantiques.com.

Page 151: Bamboo shades—Smith+Noble Window Treatments. For catalog, call 800/765-7776; www.smithandnoble.com. Adjustable swing-arm wall lamp, brass, Bestlite collection from Baldinger—GL Lites On Ltd., 1675 Third Ave., New York, NY 10128; 212/534-6363.

Pages 152–153: Faucet, Easton Lever Handle Kitchen Mixer—Waterworks, 800/899-6757; www.waterworks.com. Neon sign, 1960s—America Antiques & Design, 5 S. Main St., Lambertville, NJ 08530; 609/397-6966; www.americadesigns.com.

Page 154: Bathtub, English Steeping—Waterworks (see under Pages 152–153). Faucet #10454 Trim Large 4-Hole Roman Tub Set; hand shower #28530 Large—Hansgrohe, Inc., 800/719-1000; www.hansgrohe-usa.com. Painting—Chartreuse, State Road, Box 2350, Vineyard Haven, MA 02568; 508/696-0500.

Page 158: (Top) Leather club chairs, 1930s—America Antiques & Design (see under Pages 152–153).

RULES OF ORDER

Pages 160–171: Antique accessories throughout—English Country Antiques, Snake Hollow Road, Box 1995, Bridgehampton, NY 11932; 631/537-0606; and 21 Newtown Ln., East Hampton, NY 11937; 631/329-5773.

Page 161: Doors— La Puerta Architectural Antiques, 1302 Cerrillos Rd., Santa Fe, NM 87501; 505/984-8164. Wicker chairs, antique—Ted Meyer's Harbor Antiques, 3654 Montauk Hwy., Wainscott, NY 11975; 631/537-1442. Blue bench, vintage—El Paso Import Co., 915/532-1199; www.elpasoimportco.com.

Pages 162–163: Chairs, Patrick French Lounge Chair—Ralph Lauren Home. For nearest store, call 800/578-7656. Chair fabric #647050 Heritage—Waverly, 800/423-5881; www.waverly.com. Rattan coffee table with tray—Mecox Gardens, 257 County Rd. 39A, Southampton, NY 11968; 631/287-5015. Wrought-iron candelabra—Connie Pentek Designs, 877/691-3049; www.pentekdesigns@bigplanet.com. Santos—Gloria List Design Center, 418 Cerrillos Rd., Santa Fe, NM 87501; 505/982-5622. Candles—Colonial Candles. For nearest dealer, call 800/343-4534; www.colonialathome.com. Painting—Throckmorton Fine Art Inc., 153 E. 61st St., 4th Floor, New York, NY 10021; 212/223-1059. Blue bench, vintage—El Paso Import Co. (see under Page 161).

Page 165: Sofa #145-003M-S—Mitchell Gold, 800/789-5401; www.mitchellgold.com. Floral pillow, Guinevere—Ralph Lauren Home (see under Pages 162–163). Leopard pillow, antique—Laura Fisher/Antique Quilts & Americana, 1050 Second Ave., Gallery 84, New York, NY 10022; 212/838-2596.

Page 167: Silver box #SB01B—Jo-Liza International, 877/456-5492; www.joliza.com.

Page 168: (Right) Jewelry—Barbara Trujillo Antiques, 2466 Main St., Box 866, Bridgehampton, NY 11932; 631/537-3838.

Page 169: Standard shams, Bromley Lace; Euro sham, Bartlett; quilt, Bartlett—Ralph Lauren Home (see under Pages 162–163). Serape—Laura Fisher/Antique Quilts & Americana (see under Page 165). Santos, milagros—Gloria List Design Center (see under Pages 162–163). Silver frame #SF65—Jo-Liza International (see under Page 167). Lamp, antique—The American Wing, 2415 Montauk Hwy., P.O. Box 1131, Bridgehampton, NY 11932; 631/537-3319.

Page 170: Silver vase—Gloria List Design Center (see under Pages 162–163).

Page 171: (Bottom right) Leather case—Cowboys and Indians Antiques, 4000 Central Ave., SE, Albuquerque, NM 87108; 505/255-4054; www.collectorsguide.com/cowboys.

MELTING POT

Page 174: Ottoman #1906-88 Victorian Bench—Hickory Chair Co., 800/349-4579; www.hickorychair.com. Ottoman fabric, Kilimanjaro Tapestry, blue/off white—Brunschwig & Fils, Inc., 212/838-7878; www.brunschwig.com; to the trade (interior design professionals only; contact a local interior designer for help with purchasing). White upholstery fabric, Brandywine Duck—Calico Corners, 800/213-6366; www.calicocorners.com. Seagrass carpet—Almar Carpet, 800/497-2562.

Page 175: Daybed upholstery fabric #P310-0053 Oyster/Blue Stripe—Euro Linens West, 888/892-1238.

Pages 176–177: Chairs #69 Rose Dining Chair; #99 Rose Armchair—Swedish Blonde, 800/274-9096; www.swedish-blonde.com. Wall paint #1A13-4 Buttercorn, Behr Premium Plus—Home Depot. For nearest store, visit www.homedepot.com.

Page 178: Lamp, Spy Lamp—Artemide, 631/694-9292; www.artemide.com. Fish wall hanging—Paula Hamilton By Hand, 520/623-5343.

Page 179: Wall paint #2B37-2 Passive Purple, Behr Premium Plus—Home Depot (see under Pages 176–177). Bench, The Louis XVI Sofa, caned back and seat—The Louis Collection. For nearest retailer, call 213/763-5743. Lamp, Tolomeo—Artemide (see under Page 178).

Page 180: Sofa fabric #2095 Les Camees—Pierre Frey. For showroom information, call 212/213-3099; to the trade (interior design professionals only; contact a local interior designer for help).

Page 181: (Top) Armchair #5037-08—Hickory Chair Co. (see under Page 174). Screen—Paula Hamilton By Hand (see under Page 178).

PERSONAL DESIGN STRATEGIES

Page 182: (Right) Jewelry—Barbara Trujillo Antiques, 2466 Main St., Box 866, Bridgehampton, NY 11932; 631/537-3838. Copper tray—English Country Antiques, Snake Hollow Rd., Box 1995, Bridgehampton, NY 11932; 631/537-0606.

Page 183: (Top right) Paint, walls Regal AquaVelvet, #956 glazed with Moore's Alkyd Glazing Liquid tinted with burnt umber pigment, top-coated with Benwood Flat Polyurethane; trim Satin Impervo, #956—Benjamin Moore & Co. For nearest store, call 800/826-2623; www.benjaminmoore.com. Window treatment fabric #664272 Royal Crest, topaz—Waverly, 800/423-5881; www.waverly.com. Leather chairs #5910-54, #212 vail/light brown—Hickory Chair Co., 800/349-4579; www.hickorychair.com. Black-and-tan woven throw—William A. Leinbach, The Itinerant Weaver, 356 Royers Rd., Myerstown, PA 17067; 717/866-5525. Navajo rugs, antique—Laura Fisher/Antique Quilts & Americana, 1050 Second Ave., Gallery 84, New York, NY 10022; 212/838-2596. Statue of Liberty carving—Daniel G. Strawser, 7152 Martin Creek Rd., Bloomington Springs, TN 38545; 931/858-2409; www.strawserart.com/carvings. Ship, antique—English Country Antiques (see under Page 182).

Pewter tray #964.4, pewter candelabra #1041.0—Match. Call 201/792-9444 for nearest retailer. Statue of Liberty collectibles, flag picture, antique—Barbara Trujillo Antiques (see under Page 182). Iron sconces #507 Fleur—Studio Steel Inc. (Center) Chandelier #LCT312—Lunares, 415/621-0764. Toilet #CST874 Carlyle, cotton—TOTO USA, 800/350-8686; www.totousa.com. Linen cabinet, artisan-made— Steve Reed Painted American Country Furniture, 510/233-4624. (Bottom left) Boots—Hopalong Boot Co., 3908 Rodeo Rd., Santa Fe, NM 87505; 505/471-5570.

Page 184: (Top) Railing—American Stairs & Rails, 732/363-3734. Slipcover fabric #600980 Domenica, linen—Waverly (see under Page 183, Top Right). Table #5287-50—Hickory Chair Co. (see under Page 183, Top Right). Carriage robe, antique—Laura Fisher/Antique Quilts & Americana (see under Page 183, Top Right). Silver trophy, antique—Leatherbound Antiques. For retail inquiries, contact Interiors Market, 55 Bennett St. NW, #20, Atlanta, GA 30305; 404/352-0055. Stool, antique—Barbara Trujillo Antiques (see under Page 182). Mochaware mug—Don Carpentier Pottery, 104 Mud Pond Rd., East Nassau, NY 12062; 518/766-2422.

Page 185: (Top right) Coffee table, silver bowl—English Country Antiques (see under Page 182). Native-American blanket—Laura Fisher/Antique Quilts & Americana (see under Page 183, Top Right). Lamp—The American Wing, 2415 Montauk Hwy., Bridgehampton, NY 11932; 631/537-3319. (Bottom left) Bed #140-588 Royal Country Retreats collection—Drexel Heritage Furnishings, 800/916-1986; www.drexelheritage.com. Paint, walls Regal AquaVelvet, #838 and #839 mixed 3:1; dark stripes Regal AquaVelvet, #838, glazed with Moore's Latex Glazing Liquid tinted with aquamarine blue pigment—Benjamin Moore & Co. (see under Page 183, Top Right). Curtain fabric #631970 Crewel, natural—Waverly (see under Page 183, Top Right). Other bed linens, monogrammed ottoman runner, antique—Bagley Home, 155 Main St., Sag Harbor, NY 11963; 631/725-3553. Screen, The Cottage Screen, black—Rhubarb Home, 26 Bond St., New York, NY 10012; 212/533-1817. Silver hearts (on screen)—Tesoros Trading Co, 209 Congress Ave., Austin, TX 78701, 512/479-8341.

PHOTO AND STYLING CREDITS

Pages 10–19: Photography by Reed Davis; produced by Joetta Moulden
Pages 20–29: Photography by King Au/Studio Au; produced by Mary Emmerling
Pages 30–39: Photography by King Au/Studio Au; produced by Mary Anne Thomson
Pages 40–43: Photography by Reed Davis; produced by Tricia Foley and Gary McKay
Pages 44–53: Photography by John Blais; produced by Mary Emmerling
Pages 54–63: Photography by Jeremy Samuelson; produced by Mary Emmerling
Pages 64–75: Photography by Michael Weschler; produced by Mary Emmerling
Pages 76–87: Photography by Michael Skott; produced by Ann Fox and Mary Emmerling
Page 88: Photography by Michael Donnelly; produced by Fiona Donnelly
Page 89: (Top left, center, bottom left) photography by Michael Weschler; produced by Mary Emmerling. (Top right, bottom right) photography by Michael Donnelly; produced by Fiona Donnelly
Page 90: Photography by Michael Weschler; produced by Mary Emmerling
Page 91: (Top left, top right, center) photography by Michael Weschler; produced by Mary Emmerling. (Bottom left) photography by Michael Skott; produced by Ann Fox and Mary Emmerling. (Bottom right) photography by Michael Donnelly; produced by Fiona Donnelly
Pages 92–107: Photography by Brad Simmons; produced by Joetta Moulden
Pages 108–117: Photography by King Au/Studio Au; produced by Joetta Moulden
Pages 118–129: Photography by Bill Holt; produced by Mary Emmerling
Pages 130–33: Photography by Jeff McNamara; produced by Tricia Foley
Pages 134–147: Photography by Reed Davis; produced by Mary Emmerling
Pages 148–159: Photography by Dominique Vorillon; produced by Mary Emmerling
Pages 160–171: Photography by King Au/Studio Au; produced by Mary Emmerling
Pages 172–181: Photography by Michael Weschler; produced by Paula Hamilton
Page 182: Photography by King Au/Studio Au; produced by Mary Emmerling
Page 183: (Top left, bottom left) photography by King Au/Studio Au; produced by Mary Emmerling. (Top right and center) photography by King Au/Studio Au; produced by Gary McKay and Jennifer Kopf. (Bottom right) photography by King Au/Studio Au; produced by Mary Emmerling
Page 184: (Top) photography by King Au/Studio Au; produced by Gary McKay and Jennifer Kopf. (Bottom left, right) photography by King Au/Studio Au; produced by Mary Emmerling
Page 185: (Top left and right) photography by King Au/Studio Au; produced by Mary Emmerling. (Bottom left) photography by King Au/Studio Au; produced by Gary McKay and Jennifer Kopf. (Center) photography by Reed Davis; produced by Mary Emmerling. (Bottom right) photography by Dominique Vorillon; produced by Mary Emmerling